MEDIUM ÆVUM MONOGRAPHS

EDITORIAL COMMITTEE

K.P. Clarke, G. Davies, A.J. Lappin,
S. Mossman, J. Roberts, P. Russell, C. Saunders

EDITOR FOR THIS VOLUME

A. J. Lappin

MEDIUM ÆVUM
MONOGRAPHS XLVII

NATURAL LAW

MEDIEVAL TRANSLATORS AND COMMENTATORS FACING *NICOMACHEAN ETHICS*, V.7

SHALOM SADIK

THE SOCIETY FOR THE STUDY OF MEDIEVAL
LANGUAGES AND LITERATURE

OXFORD · MMXXIV

THE SOCIETY FOR THE STUDY OF MEDIEVAL
LANGUAGES AND LITERATURE
OXFORD, 2024

http://aevum.space/monographs

© 2024 Shalom Sadik

ISBN:
978-1-911694-24-3 (PB)
978-1-911694-25-0 (HB)
978-1-911694-26-7 (E-BK)

British Library Cataloguing in Publication Data
A catalogue record for this book is available
from the British Library

*In memory of my great aunt,
Sophie Moch, who taught me
the importance of studying
foreign languages.*

CONTENTS

ACKNOWLEDGEMENTS	xiii
INTRODUCTION	xvii
Section One	xxi
Section Two	xxiv
Section Three	xxvii
Final Observations	xxvii

SECTION ONE: ARISTOTLE'S TEXT AND ITS TRANSLATIONS

1. ARISTOTLE'S TEXT, NE V.7	3
Exposition and analysis of Aristotle's text	6
I.	7
II.	8
III.	12
2. THE ARABIC TRANSLATION	21
I.	22
II.	25
III.	27
Conclusion	28
The Arabic translation of the *Nicomachean Ethics*	30

3. THE LATIN TRANSLATIONS	31
I.	32
II.	34
III.	36
Conclusion	37
The Texts of the Latin Translations	39
Grosseteste's and Moerbeke's Translation	39
Leonardo Bruni's Translation	40
4. THE HEBREW TRANSLATIONS	43
Rabbi Meir Alguadez	43
Rabbi Baruch ben Yaish	47
The texts of the Hebrew Translations	50
Rabbi Alguadez's Translation	50
Rabbi Baruch's Translation	51
CHAPTERS 1-4: SUMMARY	53
5. AVERROES' *COMPENDIUM* (MIDDLE COMMENTARY)	55
The translations of Averroes	66
I.	66
II.	67
III.	67

SECTION TWO:
MEDIEVAL COMMENTARIES

6. GREEK BYZANTINE COMMENTARIES ... 71

The anonymous commentator ... 72
    I. ... 73
    II. ... 75
    III. ... 77

Michael of Ephesus ... 81
    I. ... 81
    II. ... 82
    III. ... 83

Georgios Pachymeres ... 86
    I. ... 87
    II. ... 88
    III. ... 88

Conclusion ... 90

Texts of the Byzantine Commentators ... 93
    The anonymous commentary ... 93
    Michael of Ephesus ... 96
    Georgios Pachymeres ... 100

7. LATIN COMMENTARIES ... 103

Albertus Magnus ... 104

Thomas Aquinas ... 116
    I. ... 118
    II. ... 122
    III. ... 123
    Conclusion ... 125

Radulphus Brito ... 126

Geraldus Odonis ... 130

Conclusion	132
Texts of the Latin commentators	134
Albertus Magnus	134
Thomas Aquinas	143
Radulphus Brito	150
Geraldus Odonis	153

8. THE HEBREW COMMENTARIES — 161

Rabbi Joseph Ibn Kaspi	162
Rabbi Joseph Ibn Shem-Tov	164
I.	164
II.	166
III.	168
Rabbi Baruch Ibn Yaish	169
I.	170
II.	171
III.	172
Summary	175
Texts of the Hebrew commentaries	178
Trumat HaKessef (The Donation of Silver)	178
The commentary of Joseph Ibn Shem-Tov	172
Rabbi Baruch Ibn Yaish's commentary	172

9. CONCLUSION — 189

Relativism	190
Non-relativists	191
Conclusion	197

SECTION THREE

9. NATURAL LAW IN MEDIEVAL JEWISH PHILOSOPHY: A SUMMARY — 201

   1. Natural law as identical to the divine commandment — 207

   2. Natural law with a distinction between rationally understandable and non-understandable commandments — 208

   3. Natural law as a minor reason to practice the commandments — 209

   4. Natural law as a reason to practice only some of the commandments — 210

   5. Relativist moral opinion with an historical advantage to the Jewish commandments — 211

   6. Relativist opinion — 209

   Conclusion — 190

BIBLIOGRAPHY — 215

   Primary sources — 215

   Other sources — 217

   Secondary sources — 218

ACKNOWLEDGEMENTS

Firstly, I must express my gratitude to God, who has granted me the opportunity to dedicate my life to learning and teaching philosophy. I hope that this book, among many others, will contribute to the understanding that deeply religious thinkers can also be great, critical, and original philosophers—an idea often criticized by the prevailing secular trend in the Western academic world. All the medieval thinkers we analyse in this book are deeply religious, including Muslims, Christians, and Jews. They believe that the study of Aristotle's Ethics is not only a part of their philosophical inquiry but also integral to their religious journey in understanding human beings and society as a means to comprehend God's creation and promote more *loving-kindness, righteousness, and justice on earth* (Jeremiah 9, based on the interpretation of Maimonides in Guide of the Perplexed III: 54). I hope and pray that more philosophers and academic scholars will continue to tread the paths laid out by these great medieval thinkers.

I worked on this book while serving as an associate professor in the Goren Goldstein Department of Jewish Thought at Ben Gurion University of the Negev. I would like to express my gratitude to the students and faculty members of the department for creating a wonderful and intellectually stimulating environment that is both supportive and enriching. A special acknowledgment is owed to my thesis supervisor, Professor Daniel Lasker, whose vast knowledge, academic expertise, and guidance have been invaluable throughout my career, even more than fourteen years after I completed my PhD. He will always serve as an exemplary model for me of how an academic scholar and mentor should conduct themselves.

Several individuals provided invaluable assistance in the writing of this book. Dr David Rundle deserves special mention for proposing the idea of expanding an article into a book and facilitating the connection between myself and Professor Anthony Lappin, the editor of Medium Ævum Monographs. Professor Lappin collaborated with me on this book, offering crucial assistance and guidance that went beyond traditional editorial duties. His input not only made the writing process enjoyable but also significantly expedited it. Professor Lappin meticulously reviewed the manuscript multiple times, providing feedback that enhanced the quality of my work. Additionally, Professor Lappin facilitated introductions to Lapo Lappin (his son), who assisted with English editing, and Robert Andrews, who provided major support in transcribing Latin commentaries and translations. It has been a pleasure to collaborate with such a talented team, and I am grateful to them for their contributions to the publication of this book.

Finally, I would like to express my heartfelt gratitude to my family. To my parents, Jaque and Chantal Sadik, who raised me in an environment rich with academic and intellectual stimulation. To my two sisters, Myriam Safrai and Deborah Schwartz, who have been integral parts of my life since their births. To my children and daughter-in-law: Yaakov and Noa, Maayan, Ayal, Naama, Ilan, Nitsan, Eliyah, Hadar, Hadas, Tehila, and Reut. My children are the greatest project and source of satisfaction in my life. Watching them grow has been a pleasure, and being a father has undoubtedly been the best preparation for a deep understanding of Aristotle's ethics. To my wife, Navit, the love of my life, who always listens attentively to my philosophical ideas and projects. Her loving yet incisive critique has greatly helped me focus on the right projects and has made my thoughts clearer and more consistent. Without her support, I would never have been able to dedicate my life to teaching and learning philosophy. אשת חיל מי ימצא (Proverbs 31: 10). I thank God that I found her.

בַּיִת וָהוֹן נַחֲלַת אָבוֹת וּמֵה' אִשָּׁה מַשְׂכָּלֶת:

A house and wealth are an inheritance from fathers, But an intelligent woman comes from the LORD (Proverbs 19: 14).

INTRODUCTION

The aim of this book is to conduct a thorough analysis of the various medieval translations and commentaries of Aristotle's *Nicomachean Ethics* V.7 (1134b-1135a). This chapter is of particular importance as it elucidates Aristotle's opinion on the concept of natural law, a highly contested topic in medieval, as well as modern, philosophy. Through an examination of the various translations and commentaries of this passage, we can observe the diverse medieval interpretations of Aristotle's stance on natural law.

The concept of natural law and its relation to other Aristotelian opinions, especially the doctrine of the mean, is a very extensive subject. It goes beyond the scope of this book to describe the history of these concepts in the different medieval traditions.[1] Another significant aspect to consider is the relationship between natural law and

---

[1] Several works have delved into this subject, particularly within the Western Christian tradition, including Fuchs 2017, Saccenti 2001. For insights into the diverse perspectives of Jewish medieval philosophers, refer to: Novak 1998; Jacobs 2010; Sadik forthcoming. In the latter work, I critique previous studies in Jewish philosophy, arguing that they overly focus on a limited set of thinkers and prioritize the exposition of individual views rather than conducting a thorough historical investigation. I believe that this criticism also applies to existing literature on Muslim philosophy. Additionally, there is a book that compares various traditions on this subject: Emon, Levering and Novak 2014.

human right.[2] I align more closely with the view presented by Strauss.[3] In my view, there is not necessarily a connection between natural law and human right. The concept of natural law can exist independently, without implying the existence of human rights. Philosophers, such as Plato in the *Republic* can conceive of natural law without positing that individual humans possess inherent human rights. Conversely, the assertion of human rights requires a belief in the existence of natural law. To argue for the existence of human rights, philosophers must first affirm the presence of some form of natural law and subsequently contend that this natural law entails certain human rights. However, I contend that none of the thinkers analysed in this book hold such a position. I will therefore not provide a discussion of the question of natural rights within the scope of this work.

For these reasons the aim of this book is to focus on a more limited subject: the way that translations of and commentaries on a specific chapter of the *Nicomachean Ethics* influence and expose the different ways of understanding the question of natural law. This is a limited but important subject that can show both the historical development of this subject in medieval philosophy and the importance of a deep study of translations to understand the way that medieval thinkers understand Aristotle. In our day and age, scholars tend to use modern editions of Aristotle, even when they want to interpret the medieval authors. In some cases, these

---

[2] On this matter, see Tierney 2001.
[3] Strauss 1999.

modern translations are very different to the medieval translation that the medieval thinkers use.

Another important aspect is to show the deep relation between the three different religions and traditions of interpretation of Aristotle in the medieval period. The Arabic translation has some influence on Jewish and Muslim thinkers. The *Compendium* of Averroes also had a deep influence on Jewish and Christian thinkers. By the end of the medieval period, we will also show that the Christian translators and commentators (especially Thomas Aquinas) have a deep influence on the Jewish translators and commentators. In our analysis, we will observe that Byzantines developed a distinct approach to understanding Aristotle's work, which notably diverges from the Latin commentators' perspective.

The history of natural law in Latin Christian philosophy differs considerably from that of Muslim and Jewish philosophy. Amongst the Latin, following the Stoa[4] and Cicero,[5] the question of natural law was an important subject within the field of ethics. In the chapter dedicated to Latin commentators, it will become evident that Cicero exerts a discernible influence on the Western medieval comprehension of this subject, by asserting that conventional law derives its basis from natural law. Interestingly, this perspective is also embraced by

---

[4] For a comprehensive examination of the significant impact of Stoicism on the subsequent evolution of Western philosophical thought concerning natural law, please refer to Fuchs, specifically pp. 68-72.

[5] Regarding this matter, please consider especially Cicero, De republica III; De legibus I-III. On the opinion of Cicero on this subject see Asmis 2008.

Averroes, who likely arrived at this viewpoint independently, devoid of any direct influence from the Roman philosopher. Both the direct influence of Averroes and the indirect influence of Cicero will hold significant sway over the Jewish commentators as well. By contrast, in Arabic philosophy (including Jewish philosophy until the fifteenth century),[6] there are no analyses or studies dedicated explicitly to this question.[7] We cannot explain all the history behind this major difference between Latin and Arabic philosophy in this book. However, we will show how the understanding of a very important text of Aristotle varied, at times significantly, according to the differing opinions on natural law held by the thinkers and translators who considered the text.

[6] To delve into the evolution of Jewish philosophy on this subject, examine: Guttman 1955; Lerner 1964; Sagi 1998, pp. 123-125; David 2010; Ehrlich 2006; Fox 1972; Melamed 1986; Rudavsky 2012.

[7] In Arabic there is no specific term for natural law and morality. We will see, however, that natural justice لطبيعة العادلة indeed exists in Arabic writings, albeit not as an important subject within ethics. To understand what a philosopher like Al-Farabi, Averroes, or Maimonides, have thought on this subject, we are required to juxtapose their writings where we find apparent inconsistencies which have led to divergent opinions regarding their actual positions on various topics. For example, the opinion of Maimonides in the eighth chapter of the treatise on logic stands in contrast to his opinion in chapter II.39 of the *Guide of the Perplexed*. The same contrast exists in the writing of Al-Farabi between what he wrote in chapter 33 of *'Ara' ahl al-Midnia al-Fadilah* (*Opinions of People of the Perfect State*). In other writings, Al-Farabi assumes that there are some religious laws that are better than others: *Kitab as-Siysah al-Madinyah* (translated as *Public Administration*) chapter 3 (p. 181 of the bilingual French translation, Al-Farabi 2012).

Section One

In the initial chapter of this book, we will provide passages from the Greek text of Aristotle's *Nicomachean Ethics* and offer interpretations thereof. It will become apparent that there are internal tensions within this chapter, which subsequently led some translators and commentators to strive for a greater consistency in Aristotle's opinions than is found in the original text. Throughout this chapter, I will also record, in the accompanying footnotes, the divergent approaches taken by contemporary scholars in interpreting Aristotle. It becomes evident throughout the book that medieval translators and commentators share important similarities with modern interpretations, highlighting the significance of medieval translations and commentaries in deepening our understanding of Aristotle. Regrettably, many contemporary scholars often overlook or disregard the medieval interpretations of Aristotle, failing to recognize the long history of medieval (and even classical) understanding that underlies the differing modern interpretations of Aristotle.

In the next three chapters of the first section, we will undertake an analysis of the various medieval translations of Aristotle's *Ethics*. The second chapter will be on the Arabic translation by Ishaq b. Hunain. The third chapter will be dedicated to an examination of the first Latin translation by Grosseteste and William of Moerbeke.[8]

---

[8] Regarding the philosophical implications of Grosseteste's translation and its influence, see Poblete 2018 and 2020. The latter conducts a thorough analysis of the philosophical implications of Grosseteste's translation and its influence on the thought of Albertus Magnus and Thomas Aquinas. Poblete also conducts

Additionally, we will summarize the minor differences between this translation and the subsequent Latin translation by Leonardo Bruni. The fourth chapter we will explore two Hebrew translations, namely: 1) Meir Alguadez's translation into Hebrew of the first Latin translation of the *Ethics* by Grosseteste, as revised by William of Moerbeke, and 2) Baruch Ibn Yaish's Hebrew translation of Leonardo Bruni's humanist Latin rendering. Throughout these translations, our focus will be on the distinctive variations between the original Greek text and each specific translation.

In these chapters, we will examine how certain translators have rendered the *Ethics* in a more relativistic

---

a comparative analysis of Grosseteste's translation and the sole surviving source of an earlier Latin translation, a manuscript that incorporates certain modifications to Grosseteste's text, influenced by that prior Latin translation (Poblete 2018, n. 16). Furthermore, Poblete meticulously scrutinizes the original text by Grosseteste and the alterations introduced by Moerbeke. Notably, Poblete's focus is primarily on the Latin tradition, specifically Grosseteste's translation, and he conducts an in-depth analysis within this context. Consequently, in the scope of my analysis, my effort will focus on Grosseteste's translation, including the modifications by Moerbeke. This study will place a particular emphasis on the comparative examination of this translation with its Arabic and Hebrew counterparts. My conclusion resonates with Poblete's observation that Grosseteste's translation contributed significantly to shaping the subsequent Latin tradition, promoting the concept of a distinct natural law, which bears influences from figures like Cicero and Stoic philosophy. Nevertheless, there are some nuanced differences in my analysis compared to Poblete's interpretations of certain passages.

manner compared to the original Greek text. This inclination is particularly evident in the Arabic translation and in the Hebrew translation by R. Alguadez. Conversely, the first Latin translation tends to present the text in a slightly more favorable light towards a natural law perspective. The second Latin translation and the Hebrew translation by R. Baruch, which is based on it, effectively convey the internal tensions present in the original Greek text.

It is important to clarify that when referring to the relativist view, I do not intend to imply a position that dismisses the existence of moral obligations. Instead, I am referring to a view that asserts that objective morality varies based on geographical locations and cultural or historical contexts. According to this perspective, there exists a morally correct course of action for each unique place and situation, whilst moral principles and legal codes must adapt to accommodate different contexts. In accordance with this perspective, a Mongol warrior, a samurai, and a medieval knight would be expected to behave quite differently from each other, but there always remains one morally right course of action for each of them within their respective contexts.

In the fifth chapter, we will undertake an analysis of Averroes'[9] *Middle Commentary* (or *Compendium*) on this

---

[9] On Averroes, see Urvoy 1988. Regarding his opinion on natural law, see Taliaferro 2017. On the translation of Averroes in Hebrew, see also Halper 2010. In his research, Halper analyses the differences between the Arabic translation of the Metaphysics and the original Greek, as well as the Arabic original and the Hebrew translation of Averroes' commentary.

section of the *Ethics*.[10] Unfortunately, the original Arabic text of the commentary is mostly lost to us.[11] Therefore, we will rely on the Hebrew and Latin translations of this compendium, quoting and examining them extensively. Averroes' commentary holds significant importance as it exerted a substantial influence on Hebrew and Latin translations and commentaries of Aristotle's *Ethics*. Samuel ben Judah's Hebrew translation of Averroes' *Middle Commentary on the Ethics*, in particular, served as a primary source for Jewish thinkers seeking access to the *Ethics* prior to the emergence of later Hebrew translations based on Latin translations. The knowledge of Averroes' commentary in Hebrew translation had a considerable impact on Hebrew translators and influenced subsequent translations into Hebrew.

Section Two

The second section will be dedicated to the analysis of various medieval commentaries.

In the sixth chapter, we will examine three distinct Greek Byzantine commentaries on the *Ethics*. The first commentary is anonymous, while the second is by Michael of Ephesus, and the third is by Georgios Pachymeres. Through our analysis, we will demonstrate that these Greek commentators forged their own unique trend of interpreting Aristotle, which diverges from the parallel Latin tradition.

---

[10] This is the only commentary by Averroes on the Ethics.

[11] For an analysis of certain Arabic fragments, see Woerther, 2019. A study of this commentary is provided by Aouad and Woerther 2009.

INTRODUCTION

In the seventh chapter, we will undertake an analysis of the Latin commentators on Aristotle's *Ethics*. Our primary focus will be an examination of two prominent commentaries by Albertus Magnus and Thomas Aquinas, given the extensive scholarship dedicated to their works. This analysis will concentrate primarily upon their interpretations of the Aristotelian but will also encompass an exploration of their overarching perspectives concerning natural and conventional law. It will become apparent that Latin commentators have cultivated a distinct trend of interpretation characterized by the differentiation of various forms of natural and conventional laws. Furthermore, we will delve into the commentaries of subsequent scholars, namely Radulphus Brito and Geraldus Odonis, in order to elucidate the profound influence exerted by Thomas on subsequent commentaries. Our analysis will take in specific alterations introduced by these commentators, and thereby shed light on the evolution of interpretation within this tradition.

In the eight chapter, we will undertake an analysis of the various Hebrew commentaries on Aristotle's *Ethics*. There exist three complete medieval Hebrew commentaries for which the authors are known. The first, authored by the Maimonidean philosopher Joseph Ibn Kaspi,[12] uses the Hebrew translation of Averroes' *Middle*

---

[12] Ibn Kaspi's work takes the form of a summary of Samuel ben Judah's translation of Averroes' Middle Commentary on Aristotle's Ethics. Nevertheless, this work divulges important insights into the philosophical views and priorities of its author and it thus should, in my opinion, be described as a "commentary". Ibn Kaspi's own philosophical opinions can be identified by paying attention to important features of the work and its relation to its base text, including Ibn Kaspi's alterations

Commentary as its foundational text.[13] The second Hebrew commentary is attributed to Joseph Ibn Shem-Tov, who primarily relied on Alguadez's translation as the base text. However, Ibn Shem-Tov was also familiar with Averroes' *Middle Commentary* and incorporated its insights into his earlier writings. Additionally, he had access to the aforementioned anonymous commentary. The third commentary was likely composed by a student of Ibn Yaʿish, who drew upon the collected notes of their teacher. Naturally, this anonymous student relied on Ibn Yaʿish's Hebrew translation of the *Ethics*. Like the three translators, these three Hebrew commentators present divergent views, both in terms of their own philosophical positions and their respective interpretations of Aristotle.[14]

In the ninth chapter, we will provide a philosophical summary of the various opinions put forth by translators

of wording, his insertion of new material in certain places, and his choices about what material from the base text to include and exclude. Sackson 2016 has documented this with respect to the section of Ibn Kaspi's Terumat ha-Kesef devoted to Plato's Republic and I am of the view that his conclusions hold true equally with regards to the section dealing with Aristotle's Ethics.

[13] This is also the text that the anonymous commentator uses. There is likewise a second anonymous Hebrew commentary on the Ethics, but it is only partial, being extant in only one manuscript. See Zonta 2006, p.119, for more on this partial commentary.

[14] The book will not focus extensively on the early-modern partial commentary by Moses Almosnino. A full study of this commentary ought to be carried out as part of an examination of the continuation of Spanish Jewish philosophy in the early modern Ottoman Empire and the reception of Aristotle's Ethics in the early modern period.

and commentators of Aristotle throughout the medieval period. This summary will reveal the distinctive originality of each translator and commentator, demonstrating the presence of cultural or pluricultural influences that shape their understanding and interpretation of Aristotle's text.

Section Three

The third section, encompassing only the tenth chapter, is focused on providing a summary of the different perspectives on the concept of natural law within the context of Jewish medieval philosophy. This section essentially serves as an appendix, with the aim of offering a concise overview of this topic to readers who may not have access to the primarily Hebrew[15] primary and secondary materials on this subject.

Final Observations

It is important to note that, for the purpose of our analysis of this chapter of the *Nicomachean Ethics*, there is no differentiation made between natural law and natural justice. All translators and commentators, in harmony with my own opinion, adopt the view that when Aristotle discusses natural and conventional justice, he also includes the laws that emanate from these different forms of justice.

In the first chapter, we will provide quotations from the original Greek text as well as its modern English translation. Subsequent chapters will focus on significant

---

[15] The predominant language for philosophical works authored by Jewish scholars prior to the thirteenth century is Judeo-Arabic.

philosophical differences, quoting only the relevant passages. At the end of each chapter, we will present the entire texts in their original languages. Given that the majority of the texts closely resemble the Greek, we will not provide translations for all the versions. As regards to the commentaries, we will summarize the main differences and include selected commentaries with an English translation. At the end of each chapter, we will present the complete text of the commentaries without translation. Any notable deviation is dealt with, in any case, in the body of my analysis.

SECTION ONE

ARISTOTLE'S TEXT AND ITS TRANSLATIONS

CHAPTER ONE: ARISTOTLE'S TEXT, *NE* V.7

The connection between natural law and the doctrine of the mean is an area of contemporary debate among scholars of Aristotle. A significant aspect of this debate revolves around the interpretation of chapter 7 of book V of the *Nicomachean Ethics*. In this chapter, I will present a quotation from Aristotle's original text and provide a comprehensive analysis of its internal tensions and contradictions. Understanding these inherent tensions is crucial for comprehending the different approaches taken by medieval translators and commentators in their interpretations.

Due to inevitable limitations of length, we will be unable to provide a comprehensive exploration of the interplay between each commentator's interpretation of Aristotle's text in V.7 and their interpretation of other Aristotelian doctrines. Nevertheless, it is essential to acknowledge the correlation between the discourse on natural law and another key Aristotelian position: the doctrine of the mean.[1]

---

[1] Analyzing the various medieval interpretations of the Aristotelian doctrine of the mean (as well as the question of equity) within the confines of this study is an insurmountable task. I intend to undertake subsequent investigations focused on this subject, specifically within the medieval translations and commentaries of Aristotle.

The doctrine of the mean is one the most important and influential theories in Aristotle's *Nicomachean Ethics*.[2] According to this doctrine, a given virtue is a mean between two extremes which both constitute a corrupt version of that very virtue. For example, courage is a mean between two extreme vices: bravado and cowardice.[3] Thus, a truly courageous person should feel afraid of things that are frightening in order not to become reckless. Hence, it turns out that for everyone, conforming to this doctrine implies an understanding that virtue changes in relation to the criteria of the specific circumstances. For instance, a warrior should fight and defend his village or land, but for a child or an old woman it is legitimate, and indeed virtuous, to flee from the enemy.[4]

One may think that the above description of the golden mean is more or less complete. However, there is an intense and intrinsic connection between the mean and natural law that necessitates a clear explication of the latter before attaining a clear picture of the former. The

---

[2] On this subject see Nicomachean Ethics, II (especially chapters 6-9), III, IV, and V. There is also ample scholarly literature on this subject. See for example Urmson 1973, Curzer 1996, and Koehn 2012. These researchers defend the doctrine of the mean against the criticism of Hursthouse, 1980-1981 and Losin 1987. Without relation to this specific debate, see also Hardie 1987 and Oates 1936. This last author traces the origin of this theory to the writings of Plato and the Pythagoreans.

[3] *Nicomachean Ethics* VI.10.

[4] For another explanation of the doctrine of the mean, see Brown 1977. According to her opinion, the true mean is the same for all humankind. If people act differently, one of them is always closer than the others to the true mean.

specific focus of the question of the relation between the theory of the mean and natural law is: does the law of a given country (including its cultural norms) affect what constitutes the golden mean for the people living in that time and place?[5] For example, is it legitimate for an Mongol warrior to act completely differently to a European knight in battle, or is there one unique way to fight, which is natural and appropriate for every human society? The answer to this question depends on whether there exists some law which is perfect and conforms to human needs in all places and times, or if these needs vary according to local circumstances. There are also implications for this question depending on whether there are certain times and places that make it easier for humans to attain a virtuous way of life, which is to say that it could be that virtue is completely relative to the individual context. Can people in different societies be equally virtuous despite their living in different ways and under different circumstances? This question is also important for our understanding of society: how much of our culture is natural? How much of it depends on history or other man-made processes? These questions are a subject of major debate between historians, sociologists,

---

[5] The answer to this question is a resounding "no" for philosophers who maintain that there is one universal law that is the best regardless of any considerations such as place and time. But for those who answer "yes", a mechanism must be provided that explains how a changing law is nonetheless natural, rather than conventional.

and philosophers, and have been so for at least the last three decades.[6]

Aristotle relates to this question in the seventh chapter of the fifth book of the *Nicomachean Ethics*, 1134b-1135a. The theory of the mean is discussed in several distinct chapters in books II-V of the *Nicomachean Ethics*. However, Aristotle's opinion on natural law is revealed principally in *Ethics* V.7.[7] For this reason, his opinion on the relation between natural law and the doctrine of the mean can be amply derived from a precise and nuanced reading of this chapter. Nonetheless, in this book, we will not be focusing on Aristotle's own interpretation as such, but rather on the way that this chapter has been understood by translators and commentators in the Middle Ages, with an eye to the impact of the different cultural, societal, and religious backgrounds from which these translators and commentators hailed. Throughout this survey and analysis of the translators, we will see that the different translations altered the text of Aristotle in subtle ways that influenced the reception of Aristotle's opinion on this subject.

Exposition and analysis of Aristotle's text

We will now delve into the text to be analyzed, *Nicomachean Ethics* V.7, and specifically the first three

---

[6] Yack 1990 reviews the different interpretations of this chapter and critiques the opinion that Aristotle supports any theory of natural Law. For another interpretation of Aristotle, see von Leyden 1967.

[7] On the modern debate about Aristotle's opinion on natural law see for example Burns 2011; Corbett 2009; Duck 2020; Destree 2000.

paragraphs, as the concluding paragraphs in V.7 are not germane to our discussion. For didactic purposes, each paragraph will be presented in full, first in the original Greek, and then with the translation of W.D. Ross, with a sentence-by-sentence analysis following each of the three paragraphs.

I.

> Τοῦ δὲ πολιτικοῦ δικαίου τὸ μὲν φυσικόν ἐστι τὸ δὲ νομικόν, φυσικὸν μὲν τὸ πανταχοῦ τὴν αὐτὴν ἔχον δύναμιν, καὶ οὐ τῷ δοκεῖν ἢ μή, νομικὸν δὲ ὃ ἐξ ἀρχῆς μὲν οὐδὲν διαφέρει οὕτως ἢ ἄλλως, ὅταν δὲ θῶνται, διαφέρει, οἷον τὸ μνᾶς λυτροῦσθαι, ἢ τὸ αἶγα θύειν ἀλλὰ μὴ δύο πρόβατα, ἔτι ὅσα ἐπὶ τῶν καθ' ἕκαστα νομοθετοῦσιν, οἷον τὸ θύειν Βρασίδᾳ, καὶ τὰ ψηφισματώδη.

> Of political justice, part is natural, part legal; natural, that which everywhere has the same force and does not exist by people's thinking this or that; legal, that which is originally indifferent, but when it has been laid down is not indifferent, e.g. that a prisoner's ransom shall be a mina [an ancient coin], or that a goat and not two sheep shall be sacrificed, and again, all the laws that are passed for particular cases, e.g. that sacrifice shall be made in honor of Brasidas, and the provisions of decrees.

In this text, Aristotle explains that there are two aspects to political justice (πολιτικοῦ δικαίου).[8] The first one is

---

[8] I will not be analyzing the opinion of Aristotle across all his writings, and will be specifically ignoring those passages where Aristotle seems to accept the existence of natural law (see for example Rhetoric I.13-15). At some point in the future I hope to devote another study to the analysis of these problematic texts and their different translations and commentaries. For now, a proper understanding of the Nicomachean Ethics by itself is

natural (φυσικόν), and it is the same in all times and places. The second one is legal (νομικόν), and varies according to the change in legislation, time, and place. This latter type of political justice, before the act of the legislator, applies to matters that do not seem to involve a clear moral imperative, which is why conventional laws can appear to be arbitrary. This apparent arbitrariness found in conventional laws is in distinction to natural laws,[9] which are the same everywhere (πανταχοῦ) and are not relative to the acceptance of some given population. By contrast, the conventional aspects of the law derive from the decision of the legislator (though also from the unwritten acceptance of the community). In the continuation of the passage, Aristotle gives two examples of legislated laws: the exact cost of ransoming a captive; and the valuation of sacrificial animals along with other details of the sacrificial rite.

II.

Δοκεῖ δ' ἐνίοις εἶναι πάντα τοιαῦτα, ὅτι τὸ μὲν φύσει ἀκίνητον καὶ πανταχοῦ τὴν αὐτὴν ἔχει δύναμιν, ὥσπερ τὸ πῦρ καὶ ἐνθάδε καὶ ἐν Πέρσαις καίει, τὰ δὲ δίκαια κινούμενα ὁρῶσιν. Τοῦτο δ' οὐκ ἔστιν οὕτως ἔχον, ἀλλ' ἔστιν ὥς· καίτοι παρά γε τοῖς θεοῖς ἴσως

---

important because the majority of the readers of Aristotle's writings see the Ethics as presenting his true opinion, whereas they see the Rhetoric as presenting his view of the common (and errant) opinion of those very people whom the Rhetoric was intended to convince otherwise.

[9] I interpret the term "political justice" as law because Aristotle speaks here of legislation by the state. The state creates political justice by creating laws that guarantee that different individuals receive their due amount of remuneration, protection, honor, etc.

οὐδαμῶς, παρ' ἡμῖν δ' ἔστι μέν τι καὶ φύσει, κινητὸν μέντοι πᾶν, ἀλλ' ὅμως ἐστὶ τὸ μὲν φύσει τὸ δ' οὐ φύσει.

> Now some think that all justice is of this sort, because that which is by nature is unchangeable and has everywhere the same force (as fire burns both here and in Persia), while they see change in the things recognized as just. This, however, is not true in this unqualified way, but is true in a sense; or rather, with the gods it is perhaps not true at all, while with us there is something that is just even by nature, yet all of it is changeable; but still some is by nature, some not by nature.

Other modern translators provide us with alternative translations of the end of this important passage.

According to the English translation of Harris Rackham:

> That rules of justice vary is not absolutely true, but only with qualifications. Among the gods indeed it is perhaps not true at all; but in our world, although there is such a thing as Natural Justice, all rules of justice are variable. But nevertheless, there is such a thing as Natural Justice as well as justice not ordained by nature.

Compare this to Peters' translation:

> But this is not altogether true, though it is true in a way. Among the gods, indeed, we may venture to say it is not true at all; but of that which is just among us part is natural, though all is subject to change. Though all is subject to change, nevertheless, I repeat, part is natural and part not.

This translation gives the text approximately the same meaning as the translation of Ross. The French translation of Thurot is a little different:

> Mais cela n'est vrai que jusqu'à un certain point. Peut-être cette immuabilité de la justice n'existe-t-elle que parmi les

> dieux, tandis que chez nous il y a des choses qui sont naturellement sujettes au changement, quoique toutes ne le soient pas : il y a donc un droit naturel, et il y en a un qui ne dérive pas de la nature.

This last translation explains that not all things are subject to change, and in so doing resolves the contradiction created by the simple understanding of the three key elements of Aristotle's opinion, namely that: 1) all things are changeable. 2) Natural things are unchangeable. 3) There are some natural things. By limiting the applicability of the first key element, i.e. that all things are immutable, Thurot essentially negates this axiom altogether, thereby allowing room for the possibility of natural, unchanging laws.

The other French translation, done by B. Saint-Hilaire and revised by A. Gomez-Muller, offers a different rendering with the same basic meaning but more palpable.

> Cette opinion n'est pas parfaitement exacte; mais elle est vrai cependant en partie. Peut-être pour les Dieux n'y a-t-il rien de cette mobilité. Mais pour nous il y'a des choses qui. Tout en étant naturelles, sont sujettes néanmoins à changer. Pourtant tous n'est pas variable et l'on peut distinguer avec raison dans la justice civil et politique ce qui est naturel et ce qui ne l'est pas.

It is important to note that, at least in this passage, there is a difference of meaning between the modern French and English translations.

Aristotle contends that some people think that in legal matters there is no natural law because, unlike legal conventions, natural law is immutable in the same way that fire burns identically throughout every land.

According to these people, justice can only be natural if it is the same in every land and culture, i.e. is as immutable as the nature of fire. The conclusion of these people is that they do not find any cases of natural legislation. It should be noted that there is a problem with Aristotle's examples of legal conventions in that they are too clear cut to challenge the claim that all law is conventional. It is less clear, for example, whether the basic idea of ransom payments or of sacrifices is natural or merely legal convention.

According to Aristotle, this total negation of the possibility of natural legislation is not accurate, though it is true in some sense. Relative to the gods, this negation is not true at all; in the divine realm there is but one absolute truth in all matters. However, among humans, this negation is partially correct and partially incorrect. There are issues that are natural and issues that are not natural, the difference being whether the changes that invariably occur are themselves natural or not.

The looming problem in this passage is that it is relatively clear that Aristotle says that there are specific natural laws. However, it is also quite clear that he said that all things change, this being a position that goes against the definition of natural things as things that are not subject to change. The aspect that most confirms the existence of natural justice and law is found in the sentence that explains that perhaps for the gods, the belief of the people that negates natural law is completely wrong. According to this part of the chapter, it is possible that in the eyes of the gods, there is some natural domain that is not subject to change at all. Any change comes only from the human perception of justice. Convention and law can confuse human perception, but divine natural justice remains in the minds of the gods.[10]

III.

Ποῖον δὲ φύσει τῶν ἐνδεχομένων καὶ ἄλλως ἔχειν, καὶ ποῖον οὒ ἀλλὰ νομικὸν καὶ συνθήκῃ, εἴπερ ἄμφω κινητὰ ὁμοίως, δῆλον. Καὶ ἐπὶ τῶν ἄλλων ὁ αὐτὸς ἁρμόσει διορισμός· φύσει γὰρ ἡ δεξιὰ κρείττων, καίτοι ἐνδέχεται πάντας ἀμφιδεξίους γενέσθαι. Τὰ δὲ κατὰ συνθήκην καὶ τὸ συμφέρον τῶν δικαίων ὅμοιά ἐστι τοῖς μέτροις· οὐ γὰρ πανταχοῦ ἴσα τὰ οἰνηρὰ καὶ σιτηρὰ μέτρα, ἀλλ' οὗ μὲν ὠνοῦνται, μείζω, οὗ δὲ πωλοῦσιν, ἐλάττω. Ὁμοίως δὲ καὶ τὰ μὴ φυσικὰ ἀλλ' ἀνθρώπινα δίκαια οὐ ταὐτὰ πανταχοῦ, ἐπεὶ οὐδ' αἱ πολιτεῖαι, ἀλλὰ μία μόνον πανταχοῦ κατὰ φύσιν ἡ ἀρίστη.

It is evident which sort of thing, among things capable of being otherwise, is by nature, and which is not but is legal and conventional, assuming that both are equally changeable. And in all other things the same distinction will apply; by nature, the right hand is stronger, yet it is possible that all men should come to be ambidextrous. The things which are just by virtue of convention and expediency are like measures; for wine and corn measures are not everywhere equal, but larger in wholesale and smaller in retail markets. Similarly, the things which are just not by nature but by human enactment are not everywhere the same, since [governmental][11]

---

[10] We can also interpret the sentence about the gods in a non-natural, legalistic way: for the gods, natural facts exist, without any conventional laws. However, humans must live in a state that has a constitution (and which undergoes other historic developments) which changes the original natural justice into a legal and non-natural one.

[11] Not in the original translation of Ross.

constitutions also are not the same, though there is but one which is everywhere by nature the best.

The opening sentence of this paragraph is as obscure as it is crucial, for its interpretation influences the understanding of the entire passage and even those that follow it. Let us therefore consider it again: Ποῖον δὲ φύσει τῶν ἐνδεχομένων καὶ ἄλλως ἔχειν, καὶ ποῖον οὐ ἀλλὰ νομικὸν καὶ συνθήκῃ, εἴπερ ἄμφω κινητὰ ὁμοίως, δῆλον ("It is evident which sort of thing, among things capable of being otherwise, is by nature, and which is not but is legal and conventional, assuming that both are equally changeable."). The translation by Ross conveys the problematic and ambiguous meaning of the Greek, for it is possible to understand this sentence in at least three different ways:

1. There are natural and legal things that are both subject to change, with the words "that both are equally changeable" (ἄμφω κινητὰ ὁμοίως, δῆλον) applying to all things, whether they be natural or conventional. According to this interpretation, Aristotle is a relativist who argues that, for example, the variation between different societies on the definition of murder speaks to the fact that there are some societies that do not forbid murder (i.e. relative to the definition of a stricter society). As such, it follows that change or variation is possible even about natural matters. A potential pitfall of this interpretation is that it seems to go against the stated position of Aristotle at the beginning of the chapter vis-á-vis the constancy of nature.

2. According to the second possible interpretation, natural things are indeed unchanging. However, the details of these things are not natural and accordingly are given to change. The words "that both are equally changeable" mean that both natural and legal things are susceptible to change, with the important distinction that natural matters can only vary in their conventional details, while purely conventional

matters can change in their entirety. What the specific restrictions on change in the natural realm might be is not at all addressed in the text, which is certainly the main problem with this interpretation. However, this interpretation makes the sentence compatible with Aristotle's earlier statements that natural things do not change. So, returning to the example of murder, this interpretation would entail that the breadth of the definition of murder can vary from one society to another, but ultimately there is a common essential basic definition of murder that is naturally forbidden everywhere, regardless of local mores and laws.

3. If we consider the continuation of the paragraph – and in particular, the example of learning to become ambidextrous – a third viable interpretation of the paragraph's first sentence arises: change can occur in natural things via human alteration of nature itself. In the example of handedness, most people could in theory choose to become ambidextrous, thereby creating a change from the original natural law. As such, this interpretation's allowance for specific kinds of change in nature qualifies Aristotle's previously stated definition of a natural law as "that which everywhere has the same force and does not exist by people's thinking this or that" (μὲν τὸ πανταχοῦ τὴν αὐτὴν ἔχον δύναμιν, καὶ οὐ τῷ δοκεῖν ἢ μή). In other words, there are certain innate abilities with which we are all born, and it is these that Aristotle described as existing independent of human volition. However, given proper human intervention, individuals or societies may change the nature of these potentially flexible abilities. According to this interpretation, murder is indeed naturally forbidden in every society. However, some societies can go against this natural tendency and allow that which nature forbids. These modifications will be deemed detrimental due to their contravention of human nature, whether human conceived as rational or social beings.

Although the three interpretations above would seem to be the only viable understandings of Aristotle's intention, there is a fourth logical possibility, albeit one that is not justified by the text as such, but nonetheless worth considering. It could be that not all laws are completely natural (because they are not universally the same the world over, like fire), nor are all laws completely conventional (because some are found universally, without regard to the actions of legislators). According to this interpretation, virtually all laws fall into a spectrum between natural and conventional, containing varying degrees of both elements, while entirely natural or conventional laws are rare.

Having completed the analysis of the first sentence of the third paragraph, we may now consider the examples brought in the middle two sentences, the first of which we already mentioned in the previous passage. We can see here that Aristotle is positing that nature is essentially what we might call the basic facts of the world (such as the right hand being stronger). At the same time, humans can change these basic facts by using their innate abilities (e.g. learning to be ambidextrous). According to the example of ambidexterity, there are certain natural facts that human intervention can change. By contrast, as the second example regarding measures demonstrates, human legislation can only influence but not actually change the basic facts of nature; being a matter of convention, measures vary according to human whim. As Aristotle notes, for example, measures in his day were larger in wholesale markets versus those used for retail markets.

The concluding sentence of the third paragraph is key for our research, though it begins innocently enough:

"Similarly, the things which are just not by nature but by human enactment are not everywhere the same, since [governmental][12] constitutions also are not the same" (Ὁμοίως δὲ καὶ τὰ μὴ φυσικὰ ἀλλ' ἀνθρώπινα δίκαια οὐ ταὐτὰ πανταχοῦ, ἐπεὶ οὐδ' αἱ πολιτεῖαι). Aristotle begins this sentence by reaffirming that things that are just and fair only according to a human standard and not naturally can vary from place to place. We have to mention that the word "enactment" in Ross's translation has no actual correspondence in the Greek original. The English translation of Rackham, "the rules of justice ordained not by nature but by man", or Thurot's French translation, "les choses qui ne sont pas naturellement justes, mais qui ne le sont qu'humainement", are in my opinion more faithful to the original Greek. These conventional things are related to human systems of government, and the changes in these systems are related to differences in place and time. This contention seems straightforward enough. However, Aristotle ends the sentence by asserting "everywhere there is one system of government that is by nature the best" (ἀλλὰ μία μόνον πανταχοῦ κατὰ φύσιν ἡ ἀρίστη). The ramifications of this statement are palpable, and thus deserve some examination.

As with the ambiguity we saw with the statement about natural versus legal mutability, we can also explain these concluding words about the existence of an ideal system of government according to two fundamentally different readings. According to the first reading, Aristotle's meaning is this: there is only one regime or

---

[12] Not in the original translation of Ross.

system of government that is in all places naturally the best. Now it follows that since government is in essence an agreed-upon social contract, i.e. convention, it follows that there is some kind of natural law that includes all kinds of legal, conventional law. Put differently, there is but one natural law on earth which suits all the historical and geographical contexts in a way that is the best according to nature. Such a natural system of government is the best system given the nature of humanity. However, geographical and historical changes can degrade that system and lead men to create an alternative political system which is less than the ideal natural system.

It is also possible that only perfect historical and geographical contexts can afford a society the possibility of attaining this ideal system of government. According to this interpretation, it is possible that some societies have no possibility of attaining this perfect political regime. For these societies, the natural system of government will be whatever the best that they can attain is. However, according to this reading, there is some kind of natural and objective point of comparison that shows that such a society is at its best and is thus as close as possible to the natural and best system of government.

The second reading of Aristotle's reference to the existence of a naturally ideal government starts with the assumption that the world everywhere (πανταχοῦ) reflects all specific different places and their particular circumstances. The meaning of the sentence would then be that in each place there is one specific system of government that is naturally the best for that place.[13]

---

[13] The interpretation of Olfert 2014 on the practical truth in Aristotle applies also to this explanation of the Greek original.

According to this reading, in each place and historical condition there exists exactly one system of government that is the best. However, there is no natural or objective criterion for determining the naturally best system of government for each place and time. For example, it is possible that a Mongol warrior must act very differently from a Japanese samurai. Nevertheless,[14] there is no natural point of comparison that can tell us which of them is acting more in accordance with natural justice. According to this interpretation, the word *nature* (φύσιν) in the phrase "that is by nature the best" relates not to the nature of each individual person, but rather to the nature of each culture or human society. Every one of these societies has a best, natural set of laws or constitution that corresponds to its specific historical background.

Without getting into a thorough interpretation of the doctrine of Aristotle,[15] a task which is not the purpose of this book, we must nonetheless pay heed to an observation that is crucial for attaining a proper understanding of the different medieval translations and commentaries: the relativist interpretation described above is closer to the apparent position of Aristotle as expressed throughout the *Ethics*, and especially in the other chapters of the fifth book. According to the absolutist interpretation, nothing is truly changeable via legislation; there is only natural justice. The only question is to what extent a specific piece of legislation is closer to

---

[14] Assuming the system of government for our hypothetical Mongol and samurai warriors is naturally the best for their distinct historical and geographical contexts.

[15] Which would require a thorough analysis of the different Greek terms used throughout the writings of Aristotle.

or further away from the singular ideal natural law. All the categories of conventional law that Aristotle constructed along with all the relativity of the way of the golden mean are completely obliterated by the assumption of an inflexible natural law. Nonetheless, we can justify the absolutist interpretation as a radical yet reasonable reading of the sentence from the middle of the second paragraph of *Ethics* V.7 which asserts that the opinion that holds that there is no such thing as natural justice is completely wrong relative to the gods.[16]

Returning to the concluding phrase of the third paragraph, "that is by nature the best", we find another important textual support for the non-relativist interpretation in that modifier *the best* (ἡ ἀρίστη). Certainly, the simplest reading of *the best* is that there exists an ideal, universally applicable legal system. On the other hand, it is tenable to interpret this superlative as referring to the best natural system of government for each society, as per the relativist interpretation. However, the non-relativist interpretation enjoys the advantage of being a more straightforward reading of Aristotle's statement that "everywhere there is one system of government that is by nature the best."[17]

In summary, while there is much material in the first three paragraphs of *Ethics* V.7 suggesting that Aristotle

---

[16] "With the gods it is perhaps not true at all" (παρά γε τοῖς θεοῖς ἴσως οὐδαμῶς).

[17] At least according to the French translation of B. Saint-Hilaire: "bien qu'il n'y en ait qu'une seul qui qui soit partout naturelle, et c'est la meilleure." The other translation of Thurot is closest to the unclear meaning of the Greek text: "mais il n'y en a qu'une seule qui soit partout conforme à la nature, et la meilleure".

allowed for a conventional aspect to otherwise natural laws, there are two arguably contradictory passages in the original Greek text which specifically lead to the more conservative interpretation that Aristotle held to a position of unchanging natural law. The first passage asserts that in the divine realm of the gods, unqualified human moral relativism is perhaps mistaken, while the second passage states that there is an ideal government in every place, potentially implying that the ideal depends on the circumstances.[18] This seeming contradiction has bothered most interpreters of Aristotle, and indeed, we will see that the Arabic translation, for example, provided a thoroughgoing revision precisely of these two passages in order to clear up the contradiction.

---

[18] There is a continuation to the chapter which may have bearing on the precise interpretation of these two passages, however this continuation is not important for our goal of clarifying how natural law is dealt with in the different medieval translations of the Nicomachean Ethics.

CHAPTER TWO: THE ARABIC TRANSLATION

In the following chapters, we will undertake an analysis of five distinct translations of the *Nicomachean Ethics* V.7. The initial translation, believed to have been composed in the ninth or tenth century, is in Arabic. The second translation, stemming from the mid-thirteenth century, is the first Latin translation, while the second Latin translation originates in the early fifteenth century. These three translations derive directly from the Greek original.

In contrast, the two Hebrew translations are based on separate Latin translations, with the first Hebrew translation also displaying traces of influence from the Hebrew version Averroes' *Compendium*. Consequently, the Hebrew translations exhibit marked distinctions from their Arabic and Latin counterparts. Nevertheless, since they nonetheless endeavour to convey Aristotle's text, and since the second Hebrew translation closely adheres to the original Greek's philosophical essence, I will examine them in the same section.

The Arabic translation was probably carried out in the ninth or tenth century.[1] The translator was likely either

---

[1] The translation of the Arabic presented here is the one executed originally by Prof. Douglas Morton Dunlop (1909–1987) of Columbia University, but which for some reason was only published posthumously in 2005 by Akasoy and Fidora, almost three decades after his passing. It is known that there are two potentially complete translations of the *Ethics* into Arabic. The

Ishaq b. Hunain (A Christian Nestorian who lived in Iraq from 808 to 873) or his father.[2] A comparison of specific texts shows that there are three major differences between the Arabic translation of this chapter and the original Greek. In all three cases, the translation steers the meaning of the passage away from the existence of an absolutist natural law in Aristotle.

I.

The first difference lies in the translation of the phrase that explains that for the gods, the opinions of those who

manuscript we possess utilizes both translations. Specifically, up to and including book V, the translation by Ishaq b. Hunain is employed. For further information on this matter, see Ullmann 2012. Dunlop's English translation is brutally literal, and no attempt was made to polish it into consistently coherent passages, nor is it known if Dunlop himself considered it a finished product. However, it is the only translation available, and certainly demonstrates an extremely professional understanding of both medieval Arabic as well as the subtleties of the original Greek text of the *Ethics*, as amply demonstrated by Dunlop's copious and meticulous annotations – annotations that, it is relevant to note, at times put the blame for the lack of coherence in the English squarely on the shoulders of the Arabic translator. Given the nature of Dunlop's translation, one may reasonably object that the Arabic, if understood less literally, might be harmonized with the Greek text. Nevertheless, we can see from the writings of those philosophers who relied solely on the Arabic translation that they generally understood it along the same lines as Dunlop. One notable exception is Averroes, and reasons for his apparent departure from the Arabic text will be provided below.

[2] The influence of the times and a number of major differences between the Greek text and the Arabic translation are discussed in *The Arabic Version of the Nicomachean Ethics* 2005, Introduction, pp. 1-109.

THE ARABIC TRANSLATION 23

reject natural law completely are likely wholly wrong. We will juxtapose the original Greek with the Arabic translation, and will provide the corresponding English translation below. Note that the initial "this" in both translations refers to the popular if misguided belief that the variation in legislation around the world demonstrates the conventional nature of all human law.

Τοῦτο δ' οὐκ ἔστιν οὕτως ἔχον, ἀλλ' ἔστιν ὥς· καίτοι παρά γε τοῖς θεοῖς ἴσως οὐδαμῶς, παρ' ἡμῖν δ' ἔστι μέν τι καὶ φύσει, κινητὸν μέντοι πᾶν, ἀλλ' ὅμως ἐστὶ τὸ μὲν φύσει τὸ δ' οὐ φύσει.	وهذا ليس كذلك، بل خليق أن يكون الذي عند الآلهة وليس هو عندنا البتّة. وهي أيضًا شيء وتحرّك بالطبع، فكلاهما [تتحرّكان]، إلّا أنّ بعضه بالطبع وبعضه ليس بالطبع.
This, however, is not true in this unqualified way, but is true in a sense; or rather, with the gods it is perhaps not true at all, while with us there is something that is just even by nature, yet all of it is changeable; but still some is by nature, some not by nature.	This is not so, but it may be that it is what applies among the gods, not among us certainly. There is also something and a movement by nature, such that both of them [vary], except that some is natural, some unnatural.

Comparing the left and right sides of the table above, we see that the meaning of this key passage changes completely in the Arabic translation. In the Greek original, Aristotle asserts that a wholesale rejection of natural law is perhaps not true regarding the gods and is only, in some sense, applicable among humans. By contrast, in the Arabic translation the opposite is the case:

among gods, the existence of natural law can be denied; however, among us humans, this negation cannot be applied. So, in short, in the Greek original, natural justice (and law) potentially includes all situations and issues, while in the Arabic translation, natural justice probably only exists among humans.[3]

The affirmation that there are both natural and non-natural (i.e. conventional) things, and that both can vary is the same in the two texts. However, there are several important differences. According to the Greek, the opinion that natural and conventional things change is only true in the human realm. But in the highest realm of truth – among the gods – there is no change in natural things. As we can see, the Greek original is most amenable to the interpretation that Aristotle accepted the existence of absolute natural law. By contrast, in the Arabic translation, the meaning of the sentence is the opposite: among gods, all things are changeable – natural and non-natural.

Another change, albeit less palpable than the one above, is in the continuation of the sentence, where it is claimed that there is variation within natural justice. This point is made more clearly in the Arabic translation. The Greek original posits that all things are mutable, some by nature and some not by nature, which is to say that change is effected via human adjudication. The Arabic translation states that there is variation in natural things.

---

[3] This understanding can explain Aristotle's application of natural law in *Rhetoric* I.13-15, as a concession to the errant human view (which does not exist among the gods) that there is some kind of natural justice and law.

In this passage, the Arabic translation makes the opinion of Aristotle more coherent than in the original Greek text. In the original, there is some contradiction between the assertion that all things change and the assertion that natural things do not change. The Arabic translation resolves this contradiction by opening up the possibility that natural justice does not truly exist (at least not in the divine ideal). For if natural justice only existed amongst humans, then it would merely be a type of subjective human perception, which would not actually reflect true nature, such that in the end, according to the truth (the opinion of the Gods) all things must change according to their relative, legal essence. Put differently, for the Arabic translator, there is no such thing as natural justice as such, but rather a category of human justice that is pervasive enough to appear to be natural to some people.

II.

The next change made by the Arabic translator that we shall examine relates to the beginning of the third paragraph of *Ethics* V.7, where the Greek text transitions from the second paragraph's description of the theoretical mutability of natural and conventional law and presents concrete examples to help illustrate the relevant distinctions. But before doing so, the third paragraph opens with an interesting assertion:

Ποῖον δὲ φύσει τῶν ἐνδε- χομένων καὶ ἄλλως ἔχειν, καὶ ποῖον οὒ ἀλλὰ νομικὸν καὶ συνθήκῃ, εἴπερ ἄμφω κινητὰ ὁμοίως, δῆλον

من التي يمكن أن تكون بنوع آخر أيضًا وليس بكيفية بل موافق للناموس والاتّفاق، إذ كان كلاهما يتحرّك.

| It is evident which sort of thing, among things capable of being otherwise, is by nature, and which is not but is legal and conventional, assuming that both are equally changeable. | Of the things which can be of another kind[4] also, and it is not of a certain kind but is in agreement with law and convention, since both of them vary. |

The Greek original explains that we can easily distinguish the things that change by nature from the things that change by law or convention. By contrast, the Arabic translation does not mention natural things. Indeed, while the phrase "both of them vary" in the original Greek refers to (1.) natural and (2.) legal or conventional issues, we see that in the Arabic translation, the very same phrase describes both (1.) law and (2.) convention. According to this passage in the Arabic translation, natural things do not truly exist. This is also true for the previous passage; there are only different kinds of conventional things, all of which are subject to variation.[5]

---

[4] "Can be of another kind" is equivalent to the Greek in direct English translation, which renders the same phrase as "capable of being otherwise", i.e. there is agreement here between the Greek original and the Arabic translation.

[5] We can also understand this sentence (like the French translation) as speaking only of the things that can change ("be of another kind"). This interpretation can make this sentence have a meaning that favours the existence of natural law. However, this not a good interpretation because if we take the two sentences together, we understand that the Arabic translation is not speaking of natural law because the translation *ipso facto* cancelled its true essence in the previous passage.

III.

The third and final significant alteration in the Arabic translation relates to that key last sentence of the third paragraph of *Ethics* V.7, which we analyzed earlier:

Ὁμοίως δὲ καὶ τὰ μὴ φυσικὰ ἀλλ' ἀνθρώπινα δίκαια οὐ ταὐτὰ πανταχοῦ, ἐπεὶ οὐδ' αἱ πολιτεῖαι, ἀλλὰ μία μόνον πανταχοῦ κατὰ φύσιν ἡ ἀρίστη.

وكذلك الأشياء الطبيعية العادلة إلّا أنّها تشبه وليست هي بعينها في كلّ مكان، كما أنّ سير المدينة أيضًا ليست متّفقة في كلّ مكان، بل إنّما تكون إذًا في كلّ مكان التي على الطبع فقط.

Similarly, the things which are just not by nature but by human enactment are not everywhere the same, since [governmental] constitutions also are not the same, though there is but one which is everywhere by nature the best.

And similarly, the natural just things, except that they are alike and are not the same everywhere, just as the ways of city life also do not everywhere agree, but there is everywhere one which is natural.

We can immediately spot several major differences between the two texts. First, in the original Greek, the subject of the first part was "the things which are just not by nature but by human enactment" – these things are subject to change and are not the same everywhere but change according to constitutional variation. In the Arabic translation the subject of this sentence is "the natural just things" (الأشياء الطبيعية العادلة). According to the Arabic, these things are not the same everywhere (but only "alike") and change according to the different way of life of different people. The Arabic posits that natural things also change according to the variation of laws and customs. This difference is important, because the Arabic once again goes against the notion of a universal natural law by asserting the mutability of natural things, and that these are not universal. This point dovetails well with the analysis above on the beginning of this paragraph of the *Ethics*. If natural law exists only among humans and not among the gods, then we can easily explain that this natural law changes due to its truly non-natural essence, even if this conventional essence of natural law is only perceptible to the gods.

The second discrepancy is the omission of the words *the best* at the end of the passage. In the Greek, these words ostensibly describe the fact that there is one system of government that is natural everywhere. This constitution is the best system of government possible for human beings. By contrast, in the Arabic translation, the simpler reading is that in each place there is a natural law specific to that place.

Conclusion

To summarize, the Arabic version does not change the meaning of the entire text of the *Ethics* V.7. However, through major modifications of the chapter's second and third paragraphs, this translation makes the text easier to interpret as positing that justice changes entirely relative to the variation of customs and legislation.[6] The text in the Arabic translation is more coherent, because it resolves the contradiction between the assertion that natural law exists and the observation that justice is

---

[6] It is interesting to note that this opinion offers an important similarity with the critique of natural rights by MacIntyre 1981.

changeable.[7] The Arabic translation also makes the position of Aristotle in this chapter more coherent regarding the doctrine of the mean. It is difficult to decide if the Arabic's being at variance with the Greek stems from a misunderstanding of the original by the translator, a deliberate choice to make the text more coherent, or the philosophical leanings of the translator, which push him to the text in a specific way. Ultimately, a good case can be made that these changes were made deliberately by the translator in order to resolve the internal tension between the ostensible moral absolutism of this phrase and the implicit moral relativism of Aristotle's doctrine of the mean. It is quite possible that the translator understood that he altered the text by making it more coherent with his understanding of Aristotle's overarching philosophical positions. However, it is also possible that he read Aristotle's original text *a priori* as being more coherent precisely because of his understanding of Aristotle's general position, and thus was completely unaware that despite his best intentions, his translation had altered the meaning of the original Greek text.

---

[7] In other words, something must give between the immovable signpost of natural law and the unstoppable arrow of variations in laws of justice. The Arabic translation removes the paradox by declaring the signpost to be ultimately movable after all.

The Arabic translation

Taken from *The Arabic Version of the Nicomachean Ethics*, Akasoy and Fidora (eds.) 2005, pp. 320-325.

وأمّا العدل المدني، فبعضه طبيعي وبعضه ناموسي. أمّا الطبيعي، فالذي له قوّة واحدة في كلّ مكان، ويظنّ به ذلك أو لا يظنّ. وأما الناموسي، الذي أمّا في الابتداء فليس فيه اختلاف بهذا النوع أو بنوع آخر، وإذا وضعوه فيختلف، مثل أن تكون المفاداة منا، أو أن يذبح عنزًا ولا يذبح شاتين، وجميع التي بها النواميس الموضوعة في الأشياء الجزئية مثل الذبائح. (2) وبعض الناس يرى أنّ جميع هذه تنسب إلى الحسبة من أجل أنّ أمّا الذي بالطبع [فلا] يتحرّك وفي كلّ مكان فله قوّة واحدة، مثل النار، وها هنا وعند الفرس فإن كانوا يرون أنّ الأشياء العادلة تتحرّك. (3) وهذا ليس كذلك، بل خليق أن يكون الذي عند الآلهة وليس هو عندنا البتّة. وهي أيضًا شيء وتحرّك بالطبع، فكلاهما [تتحرّكان]، إلّا أنّ بعضه بالطبع وبعضه ليس بالطبع، (4) من التي يمكّن أن تكون بنوع آخر أيضًا وليس بكيفية بل موافق للناموس والاتّفاق، إذ كان كلاهما يتحرّك وكذلك في سائر الأشياء. وبيّن أنّ هذا التفصيل يليق بها أيضًا من أجل أنّ اليد اليمنى أجود بالطبع وإن كان يمكن أن يصير جميع الناس ذا يمينين. (5) وأمّا التي تكون بالاتّفاق والذي هو أخير للعادل فإنّها تشبه الأوساط من أجل أنّ مكاييل النبيذ والحنطة ليست بمتساوية في كلّ مكان بل التي يشترى بها أكبر والتي يباع بها أصغر، وكذلك الأشياء الطبيعية العادلة إلّا أنّها تشبه وليست هي بعينها في كلّ مكان، كما أنّ سير المدينة أيضًا ليست متّفقة في كلّ مكان، بل إنّما تكون إذًا في كلّ مكان التي على الطبع فقط. (6) وأمّا نسبة كلّ واحد من الأشياء العادلة والناموسية، فكنسبة الأشياء الكلّية إلى الأشياء الجزئية، أمّا التي تفعل فكثير وأمّا كلّ واحد من تلك فواحد لأنّه كلّي. (7) وفيما بين اللا اعتدال ولا عدل، واعتدال وعدل [فاختلاف]، فإنّ أمّا لا عدل فبالطبع، وهذا بعينه إذا فعل هو لا اعتدال، ومثل ذلك الاعتدال، فإن نسمّي العامّ فعلى العدل من أجل أنّ الاعتدال يسمّى [تصحيحًا] لا اعتدالًا. وأمّا التي بنوع كلّ واحد منهما، وكم هي، وفي أيّ شيء هي، فنفحص أخيرًا عن ذلك.

CHAPTER THREE: THE LATIN TRANSLATIONS

The first Latin translation from the Greek was completed by Robert Grosseteste (Bishop of Lincoln lived between 1168-1253) around 1246-1247, and then revised shortly thereafter by William of Moerbeke (a Dominican friar born in Flanders who served as the Archbishop of Corinth, and who lived from 1215 to 1286).[1] The second Latin translation of Aristotle's work was undertaken by Leonardo Bruni (A historian and statesman who lived in Florence from 1370 to 1444.) circa 1416.

Initially, we will provide an overview of the first translation, followed by a comprehensive comparison of Bruni's translation with that of Grosseteste, focusing on each subject matter individually. In analysing how Grosseteste translates the same three paragraphs examined above, we once again encounter several departures from the Greek original, albeit fewer in number and less radical in nature. What is most notable with these changes is that they are precisely the opposite of those found in the Arabic translation. In contrast, we will observe that Bruni's translation aligns more closely with the original Greek than Grosseteste's translation. Notwithstanding the numerous linguistic divergences between these two Latin translations, I have identified two instances of substantial philosophical disparity. In these instances, Bruni

---

[1] On this translation see Poblete 2018; Poblete 2020; Callus 1947; Dunbadin 1972.

deliberately deviates from the former version in order to render his translation more faithful to the Greek original.

As with the Arabic translation, we will juxtapose the original Greek passages with their English translations alongside the corresponding passages of Grosseteste's Latin and their English translation, and then analyse the differences between the Grosseteste's Latin version and the original Greek.

I.

The first change occurs in the passage about the gods:

Τοῦτο δ' οὐκ ἔστιν οὕτως ἔχον, ἀλλ' ἔστιν ὥς· καίτοι παρά γε τοῖς θεοῖς ἴσως οὐδαμῶς, παρ' ἡμῖν δ' ἔστι μέν τι καὶ φύσει, κινητὸν μέντοι πᾶν, ἀλλ' ὅμως ἐστὶ τὸ μὲν φύσει τὸ δ' οὐ φύσει.	Hoc autem non sic habens, sed ut: quamvis apud deos nequaquam sit aliter habens. Apud nos autem est quidem aliquid natura mobile, quia quidem omne. Sed est tamen hoc quidem natura, hoc autem non natura.[2]
This, however, is not true in this unqualified way, but is true in a sense; or rather, with the gods it is perhaps not true at all, while with us there is something that is just even by nature, yet all of it is changeable; but still some is by nature, some not by nature.	However, this does not hold in this way, but is, although there is no change at all among the gods. However, among us there is indeed something that is changeable by nature, since everything, in fact, [in us] is [changeable]. Still, there is [in us]

---

[2] *Ethicorum Aristotelis*, V.12 (279).

> something by nature, indeed, and yet, something not by nature.[3]

In this passage from Grosseteste's Latin translation, we see some small deviations from the original Greek.[4] The first change is that the Latin posits in a definitive way[5] that there is no change among the gods. This is very different from the non-committal use of "may be" in the original Greek in stating that there are people that say that their non-natural justice *may be* completely wrong among the gods. Grosseteste's Latin translation provides a definitive assertion in place of the original more reserved one.

Leonardo Bruni's translation exhibits a closer alignment with the original Greek text compared to the previous Latin translation. Specifically, when translating the Greek phrase, καίτοι παρά γε τοῖς θεοῖς ἴσως οὐδαμῶς, the earlier Latin translation employs "quamvis apud Deos nequaquam sit aliter habens", whereas Bruni's reads "Enim vero apud deos quidem forsan non ita se habens." The primary distinction lies in the usage of *nequaquam* by Grosseteste and *forsan* by Bruni. Both translations remain reasonably faithful to the Greek original. However, Grosseteste presents the phrase in a

---

[3] I would like to thank Dr. Yehuda Halper of the Department of Jewish Thought of Bar Ilan University for the professional English translation he so kindly provided for this passage, as well as suggestions for the translation of the next two passages that follow in the analysis of the Latin translation.

[4] Poblete 2018, where he dedicates pages 610-611 and also 614 to the analysis of this passage.

[5] *Quamvis* (however much) in no way casts doubt on the statement about the gods, unlike the Greek ἴσως (perhaps).

definitive manner, whereas Bruni adopts a more tentative approach. In my view, Bruni's translation is closer to the original text.

Another difference is that the sentence that says that all things are changeable (κινητὸν μέντοι πᾶν) is less clear in Grosseteste's Latin translation.[6] In the Greek, the meaning is that even natural things are changeable. In Grosseteste's Latin translation, we can understand that all issues are naturally changeable ("natura mobile"). Nevertheless, this obtains only among us. Among the gods, there is no change, as we have seen. The sentence, "Sed est tamen hoc quidem natura, hoc autem non natura" ("Still, there is [in us] something by nature, indeed, and yet, something not by nature") describes the gods' point of view – that they exist as natural things which do not change and only conventional (non-natural) things are changeable. In Bruni's translation, this passage may also be interpreted as referring to the human perspective, consistent with the intention of the Greek original.

II.

This brings us to another divergence between the original Greek and both Latin translations, regarding the

---

[6] Poblete 2018, pp. 605-609, identifies additional alterations made by Grosseteste in the preceding passages. It is plausible that these modifications may have exerted some influence. However, I am of the opinion that they are too minor to yield a substantial distinction. Regarding the broader philosophical implications of Grosseteste's translation, I am in complete agreement with Poblete.

beginning of the third paragraph of *Ethics* V.7, where Aristotle attempts to distinguish between natural and conventional things:[7]

Ποῖον δὲ φύσει τῶν ἐνδεχομένων καὶ ἄλλως ἔχειν, καὶ ποῖον οὒ ἀλλὰ νομικὸν καὶ συνθήκῃ, εἴπερ ἄμφω κινητὰ ὁμοίως, δῆλον	Quale autem natura contingentium et aliter habere, et quale non, sed legale, et compositione, si ambo mobilia similiter.[8]
It is evident which sort of thing, among things capable of being otherwise, is by nature, and which is not but is legal and conventional, assuming that both are equally changeable.	Which sort of thing, among those capable of being otherwise, is by nature, and which is not but is legal and conventional, if both are similarly changeable?

The major difference between Grosseteste's Latin translation and the original Greek is that the Latin changes the passage from an affirmation to a question. The original Greek squarely rejects natural law in assuming that natural and conventional things are both changeable. The Greek asserts that it is evident that all things can be otherwise, whether they are conventional or natural. By contrast, the Grosseteste's Latin asks regarding all the things that are changeable: which of these are natural and which conventional? By changing the text from a clear assertion of the existence of purely conventional law to an open-ended question which can

---

[7] Poblete 2018, 615.
[8] *Ethicorum Aristotelis*, V.12 (279).

be answered in favour of strict natural law, Grosseteste essentially rewrites to his own philosophical liking the one text that could provide the wiggle room for an alternative reading of Aristotle as a moral relativist who does not think society must abide only by natural law. We see in the translator's analysis of the Greek text a kind of interpretation, and an important one at that. The possibility is raised of there being a negative answer to the question: are all things changeable? The legitimacy of this interrogative translation can be debated, but unquestionably the result is a fully consistent extended passage, with Aristotle as an unequivocal proponent of natural law. On this particular topic, Bruni shares the same opinion as Grosseteste. Both translators employ the term *quale* to convey their interpretation.

III.[9]

The main divergence lies in the third passage following the example of ambidexterity. According to Aristotle, all individuals have the potential to become ambidextrous. However, Grosseteste omits the word *all*, as illustrated in the table below:

καίτοι ἐνδέχεται <u>πάντας</u> <u>ἀμφιδεξίους γενέσθαι.</u>	Natura enim dextra melior, quamvis contingit ambidextros fieri.[10]
By nature, the right hand is stronger, yet it is possible	By nature the right hand is better, although it is possible

---

[9] See Poblete 2018, 611.

[10] According to Poblete 2018, p. 611, the Latin of Grosseteste also includes the word 'fieri'.

| that <u>all men</u> should come to | to become ambidextrous. |
| be ambidextrous. | |

This alteration carries significant importance since, in Aristotle's view, all things possess the capacity to deviate from their natural state. Conversely, Grosseteste's translation implies that while certain entities can undergo change, it is also plausible that there are things which cannot deviate from their natural condition. This constitutes the primary modification introduced by Grosseteste, intended to bolster the interpretation that there exists a form of natural law immune to alterations.

In this passage, Bruni's translation closely adheres to the Greek original and includes the word omitted by Grosseteste: "Natura enim dextra melior est, fieri potest tamen ut omnes ambidextra sint."

Conclusion

In analyzing Grosseteste's Latin translation we see that it is nearer to the Greek original than the Arabic one. However, as with all translations, and especially the medieval ones, there is some change in the meaning of the text. The changes made in the Latin translation reflect a specific style of interpretation. They make the text more amenable to being interpreted as asserting the existence of an absolute natural law than the original Greek does, while the Arabic translation tends in the opposite direction.

It is probable that both Latin translators were influenced by their knowledge of Cicero and other early Christian writers who followed him in speaking of natural law. It is also possible that they were simply influenced by their own philosophical opinions or by their personal understanding of Aristotle. What is certain is that the various thinkers who read Aristotle in Grosseteste's Latin or Arabic translation essentially read two different Aristotles, which in turn influenced the two traditions differently. By contrast, Bruni likely made a slight alteration in the meaning of the text to align it more closely with the Greek.[11] Interestingly, Bruni's translation may lean slightly towards favouring natural law compared to that Greek original.

---

[11] For an overview of Bruni as translator, see Le Blanc 2008 and Botley 2004.

The texts of the Latin translations

Grosseteste's and Moerbeke's translation

I.

Politici autem iusti hoc quidem naturale est, hoc autem legale. Naturale quidem quod ubique habet eamdem potentiam, et non in videri, vel non. Legale autem quod ex principio quidem nihil differt sic vel aliter. Quando autem ponitur differt, puta mina redimi, vel capram sacrificare, sed non duas oves. Adhuc, quae in singularibus lege ponunt, puta sacrificare Brasidae, et sententialia.

II.

Videtur autem quibusdam omnia esse talia. Quia quod quidem natura immobile, et ubicumque eamdem habet potentiam, quemadmodum ignis, et hic et in Persis ardet. Iusta autem mota conspiciuntur. Hoc autem non sic habens, sed ut: quamvis apud deos nequaquam sit aliter habens. Apud nos autem est quidem aliquid natura mobile, quia quidem omne. Sed est tamen hoc quidem natura, hoc autem non natura.

III.

Quale autem natura contingentium et aliter habere, et quale non, sed legale, et compositione, si ambo mobilia similiter. Manifestum, et in aliis eadem congruit determinatio. Natura enim dextra melior, quamvis contingit ambidextros. Quae autem, secundum compositionem, et conferens iustorum, similia sunt mensuris. Non enim sunt ubique aequales vini et frumenti mensurae. Sed ubi quidem emuntur, maiores, ubi autem venduntur, minores. Similiter autem, et non naturalia, sed humana iusta non eadem ubique, quod neque urbanitas. Sed una solum ubique secundum naturam optima.

Leonardo Bruni's translation

I.

Ius alterum naturale est, alterum legitimum. Naturale quod ubique eandem habet vim, non quia sic videatur vel non. |1134b20| Legitimum quod nihil ab initio referebat hoc vel illo modo esset, sed postquam lata est lex refert veluti ut redemptiones captivorum certo pretio fiant, utque capra immoletur, non duae oves, et quae de singulis cauta legibus sunt, ut sacra facere Brasidae, et decreta publica.

II.

Videntur autem quibusdam cuncta esse eiusmodi, |1134b25| nam quod naturale est, id immutabile est, et ubique eandem habet potestatem, ut ignis hic et in Persis urit. Iura vero mutari videntur; hoc autem non est ita se habens, sed sic. Enim vero apud deos quidem forsan non ita se habet, apud nos certe aliquid est |1134b30| naturale, mutabile non omne quidem, sed tamen est aliud natura, aliud non natura,

III.

quale autem natura se aliter habere potest, et quale non, sed lege ac positione si quidem utraque mutabilia similiter manifestum est, in aliis quoque eadem est determinatio. Natura enim dextra melior est, fieri potest tamen ut omnes ambidextra sint. Iura vero |1135a1| secundum positionem vel utilitatem similia sunt mensuris. Non enim omnibus in locis aequales sunt tritici vinique mensurae, sed ubi emunt maiores, ubi vendunt minores. Eodem modo iura quae non sunt naturalia, sed humana non eadem sunt ubique, nam neque res patet, sed una dumtaxat ubique secundum naturam optima.

CHAPTER FOUR: THE HEBREW TRANSLATIONS

Apart from the translation of the *Compendium* (*Middle Commentary*) of Averroes by Samuel son of Yehuda, which will be analyzed in the next chapter, there exist two Hebrew translations, based on two different Latin translations (but also influenced by the *Compendium*).

Rabbi Meir Alguadez

The first translation was by Rabbi Meir Alguadez, the chief Rabbi of Castile (d. 1410).[1] This translation of the *Ethics* was popular and survives in seventeen manuscripts.[2] Rabbi Alguadez used as the main source for his translation the widely known thirteenth-century Latin translation by Robert Grosseteste, revised by William Moerbeke, which we have discussed above. As will be seen below, Rabbi Alguadez's translation contains significant departure that do not originate from the Latin source – and thus Grosseteste's Latin is closer to the Greek original than this Hebrew translation. Furthermore, it is noteworthy that the philosophical significance

---

[1] On this translation see Berman 1988 and Neria 2015, pp. 383-409. Neria gives an edition of the translationpp. 411-566. On the introduction to this translation, see also Rothschild 2016 and 2011.

[2] This translation is also fully preserved in some of the manuscripts, including the commentary by Rabbi Joseph Ibn Shem-Tov, which we will address later.

of Alguadez's departure from the Greek original proceeds in a direction contrary to that of his Latin source.

There are multiple ambiguous meanings in Rabbi Alguadez's translation, just as in the original Greek and Grosseteste's Latin. Nevertheless, some of these ambiguous meanings differ from Alguadez's sources due to a series of significant changes made in his translation. In our analysis of this translation, we will summarize these major changes and focus on their philosophical import.

As regards the first paragraph, the translation is quite similar to his Latin source (and the Greek original): natural justice is the same everywhere; in contrast, conventional (or legal)[3] justice stems from the fact that "a division was placed in it" (שהושם יש בו חילוק,) meaning it was decided to be so and not otherwise—and after this decision, it must be upheld. The examples of sacrifices are also identical to his source in Greek and Latin.

In the beginning of the second paragraph there is a small alteration: the negation of the assertion by "some people" who deny the existence of a natural justice is not explicit. The phrase, אמנם נראה שאינו כן אבל הוא (though it seems not so, yet it is) can easily be continued with the addition of "thus it is", which would express agreement with their statements that undermine natural morality. Here, too, there is no connection between Rabbi Alguadez's translation and its Latin source: "Hoc autem non sic habens, sed ut ..." (though it is not so, yet...). Rabbi Alguadez adds the word, נראה (seems) which introduces some doubt into the negation.

---

[3] He uses the Hebrew word דתי that can mean *legal* but also has the meaning of *religious*.

The main difference in the second paragraph is found latter: instead of distinguishing between the viewpoint of God, which remains unchanged, and the viewpoint of humans, which changes, Rabbi Alguadez writes: כי אף על פי שהדברים האלוהיים הם קיימים וחזקים ("even though the divine matters exist and are strong"). Here too, there is no influence from the Latin translation, which reads: "quamvis apud Deos nequaquam sit aliter habens" similar to the Greek original. Rabbi Alguadez's translation can be understood in two different ways. Firstly, it can be understood as being close to the source: divine matters mean those spoken from a divine perspective, while "matters with us" are perceived from a human perspective. This can also be understood differently: "the divine matters" refer to divine subjects such as metaphysics (the divine science), while "the matters with us" refer to human matters, namely ethics. According to this second interpretation, only metaphysics does not change in every society, while ethics is "entirely subject to nature", meaning even natural matters in ethics change.

At the beginning of the third paragraph, there are slight changes, but they do not significantly alter the philosophical import of the text. According to this passage, Rabbi Alguadez also acknowledges the existence of natural justice, which is the initial state of human society, and religion (rather than law in a strict sense) improves the natural state by adding legal or religious laws. In the complex sentence at the end of the paragraph, there is a slightly more significant difference in meaning. The sentence in Rabbi Alguadez's translation states:

But matters (that are related to) human justice are not the	אבל הדברים האנושיים ישרים אינם שווים בכל מקום, באנשי

same everywhere; the manners of city dwellers are not the same. However, they are the same in each place as nature dictates.	ישוב המדינות אינו שוה אבל הוא אחד לבד בכל מקום כפי הטבע נבחר.

This sentence can be more easily understood as supporting a relative morality. There is a "natural justice" that differs in each places according to the specific conditions of each specific place, meaning that in each place there is a natural morality that arises from the nature of the place. Here too, there is no influence from Grosseteste's Latin source: "Sed humana justa non eadem ubique, quod neque urbanitas, sed una solum unique second naturam optima."

It can be concluded that Rabbi Alguadez's translation allows for a more easily readable interpretation that supports a relative morality that varies according to the place, as opposed to divine matters, namely the metaphysical aspects that exist everywhere. Such an interpretation is also based on the Greek source. It is also not the only possible reading in Rabbi Alguadez's text, but it nonetheless remains a live option, for him more than in any other known source.[4] Grosseteste's Latin translation, which served as his source, notably went in

---

[4] This is also the significance of the changes made by the Arabic translation. However, the changes are not similar, so I do not believe it is possible to show that the Arabic translation influenced Rabbi Alguadez. There is, further, no indication that Rabbi Alguadez knew Arabic or that anyone in his surroundings was familiar with the Arabic translation. It is most likely, then, that both translators aligned the text in the same direction because they thought it was Aristotle's position, without any connexion between them.

the opposite direction (albeit much more subtly). Rabbi Alguadez probably understood Aristotle as supporting a relative morality, and therefore skewed the translation in accordance with this interpretation.

Rabbi Baruch ben Yaish

Rabbi Baruch ben Yaish is credited as the author of the second translation. Little is known about Rabbi Baruch ben Yaish beyond his translated and original works. It is believed that he was active in fifteen-century Spain. One significant contribution by Rabbi Baruch ben Yaish is having providing us with the second Hebrew translation of the *Ethics*.[5] Notably, this translation directly stemmed from Bruni's new Latin translation (c. 1417). To date, only one manuscript of Baruch's translation has been discovered but there are three manuscripts containing commentaries on the *Ethics* which have been ascribed to Rabbi Baruch ben Yaish. Nevertheless, it is important to point out that these commentaries might not have been authored directly by Rabbi Baruch himself, but rather represent written records of his lectures taken down by one of his disciples.

In this chapter, we will analyse Rabbi Baruch ben Yaish's translation, while in the subsequent chapter, we will focus on the commentary. In the translation, there are minor deviations from the Greek source and the Latin source used by Rabbi Baruch. The first paragraph bears a strong resemblance, in terms of philosophical import, to that of Rabbi Alguadez. Rabbi Baruch translates the

---

[5] The central research work on this topic is Zonta's 2006, pp. 109-163. There (at pp. 155-115), Zonta provides an extensive discussion of his interpretation of the *Ethics*.

Greek term νόμος as *Daat* דת (rule or religion), likely influenced by Rabbi Alguadez's translation. There appears to be no discernible influence from Averroes' *Middle Commentary* in Hebrew. Yet unlike the Hebrew translation of Averroes, Rabbi Baruch does not employ the term נימוסי (custom) to describe non-natural legal laws. The primary distinction lies in his translation of the legal laws as מפורסמות (commonly accepted), suggesting a probable amalgamation of the influence of the Latin translation and Maimonides' views on commonly accepted commandments.[6]

In the second paragraph, Rabbi Baruch's translation is the closest to the original source among the Hebrew versions, surpassing Rabbi Alguadez's translation. This is primarily because Rabbi Baruch does not include the concept of "divine matters" ('הדברים האלוהיים) as Rabbi Alguadez does. Instead, he focuses on discussing the perspectives of both God and human beings, mirroring the approach found in the original Greek. Like the original source, with God, things do not change, and the opinion of "some of the people" (מקצת האנשים) is therefore incorrect. In contrast, from the perspective of human beings, things do change. Here Rabbi Baruch introduces one significant alteration and asserts that not everything changes. In other words, even if things change among human beings, there is still an inherent core of absolute natural morality.

In the third paragraph, Rabbi Baruch's translation remains faithful to the original source. However, we can still discern the influence of Rabbi Alguadez's translation,

---

[6] For an exploration of the significance of this term in Maimonides' *Guide for the Perplexed*, refer to Sadik 2021.

as he introduces the word "alone" (לבד) into the text. Consequently, even in Rabbi Baruch's translation, the sentence comparing civil laws tends to be understood as indicative of relative morality: in each circumstance, there exists a distinct and changeable natural morality.

In summary, it can be observed in Rabbi Baruch's translation the influence of Rabbi Alguadez's translation (the use of the word דת for legal laws and the settlement of the state), as well as the foundation derived from Bruni's Latin translation. Averroes's commentary does not exert any influence. Several other characteristics are present, including the usage of the term מפורסמות (commonly accepted). However, overall, this version is the closest to the original Greek of the Hebrew translation. This is primarily due to Rabbi Baruch using Bruni's translation to "rectify" some of the most significant changes introduced by Rabbi Alguadez. It is essential to note that the proximity of Rabbi Baruch's translation, based on Bruni, to the Greek original does not solely arise from the superiority of Bruni's translation over Grosseteste's Latin translation. It also reflects Rabbi Baruch's adherence to his Latin source while Rabbi Alguadez exercised greater freedom in his translation. In Rabbi Baruch's text, there is no attempt to reconcile internal contradictions into a coherent framework; he reserves that task for his commentary.

The text of the Hebrew translations

Rabbi Alguadez's translation

I.

הצדק המדיני ממנו טבעי וממנו דתי. הטבעי אשר הוא בכל מקום יש לו כוח שוה, ואינו תלוי בראות[7] או לא. הדתי אמנם אשר בראשונה לא יהיה בו חלוק שיהיה כן או בעניין אחר. אבל אחר שהושם יש בו חילוק, כמו שיהיה פדיון העבד שעור ידוע, או לזבוח עז ולא צאן, וגם כן הדת אשר ישימו למיוחדים, כמו לזבוח לבשאידה והדינים.

II.

יראה לקצת כי כלם הם כן, שאינם טבעיים, כי אשר הוא בטבע לא יסור, ובכל מקום יהיה לו הכח ההוא, כמו האש אשר היא שורפת הנה ובפרס, אמנם הצדקות יראה שהם נעות. אמנם נראה שאינו כן אבל הוא, כי אף על פי שהדברים האלהיים הם קיימים וחזקים, אינם כן הדברים אשר אצלנו, כי יהיה דבר טבעי נע כולו. אבל יהיה שם דבר טבעי ודבר שאינו טבעי.

III.

ועל כן אמנם טבע הדברים אשר יקרה היותם והם מתחלפים, איך נדע אלה הם בטבע ואלה לא, כי אם מצד תשומת דת, אם שניהם נעים. גלוי הוא ובשאר הדברים הטבעיים כן צריך אל ביאור. הימין בטבע הוא חזק ואם יקרה שיהיה אדם ימיני בשני

---

[7] The word ראות (seeing) is a literal translation of the Latin word *videri*. I do not understand how the Greek word δοκεῖν (knowledge, understanding) evolved into such a term in the Latin translation. Nevertheless, this translation serves as clear evidence of Rabbi Alguadez's complete reliance on the Latin translation.

צדדיו. אמנם אשר הם כפי תשומה דברים צודקים מועילים הם דומים למדות, כי אינם בכל מקום מדות היין והחטה שוות, אבל בכל מקום שהם נקנים הם גדולות, אמנם במקום אשר הם נמכרים הם קטנות. אמנם כן הם דברים בלתי טבעיים, אבל הדברים האנושיים ישרים אינם שווים בכל מקום, באנשי ישוב המדינות[8] אינו שוה אבל הוא אחד לבד בכל מקום כפי הטבע נבחר. אמנם הצדקות והדברים אשר בדת כל אחד מהם כמו הכלליים אל הפרטים, כי הדברים הנפעלים הם רבים, אבל בכל אחד מאלה יש אחד הוא אחד כולל.

Rabbi Baruch's Translation[9]

I.

היושר המדיני ממנו טבעי וממנו דתי,[10] אמנם הטבעי בכל מקום יש לו כוח א', לא כי כן יראה או לא. הדתי הוא אשר בהתחלה לא יהיה הפרש להיות כן או בענין אחר. אבל לאחר נתינת הדת יש הפרש. כמו פדיון שבוים בשיעור ידוע ולזבוח עז ולא צאן ואשר הם מדברים מיוחדים מצווים מהדתות כמו לזבוח לאבראשירה והדברים המפורסמים.[11]

---

[8] A translation of the Latin term *urbanitas*.

[9] Taken from Hamburg, Staats- und Universitätsbibliothek, ms. Levy 114, fol. 28r-v.

[10] The term הדתי (religious) undoubtedly derives from the translation of Rabbi Alguadez, and it is also written in Latin as *legitimum*, as seen in Bruni's work.

[11] The use of the term מפורסמות is intriguing, and it is reasonable to assume that it originates from Bruni's Latin translation, where he employs "decreta publica," in contrast to the first Latin translation's "sententiala." Another possibility lies in the influence of Maimonides' terminology on the translation of Ibn Tibbon, where the term משהוראת in Judeo-Arabic is translated as מפורסמות

II.

אמנם ראה לקצת כי כלם הם כן. כי הדבר הטבעי הוא בלתי משתנה, ובכל מקום יש לו כוח א', כמו האש אשר הוא שורף הנה ופרס. אכן המשפטים יראו שהם משתנים. אמנם זה אינו בזה הענין, אבל כן. הנה אמנם אצל האלוהות אולי לא יהיה כן, אכן אצלנו יהיה דבר מה טבעי משתנה <u>אמנם לא הכל</u>[12] אבל יש דבר טבעי ודבר שאינו טבעי.

III.

אמנם איך הוא אשר בטבע יכול להיות משתנה ואיך לא כי אם בדת ובהנחה אם שניהם משתנים יחד. הוא גלוי באחרים גם כן הביאור יהיה א': כי הימין בטבע הוא יותר טוב, אכן יקרה להיות אדם ימיני בשני צדדיו. אמנם המשפטים אשר הם כפי ההנחה או התועלת, הם דומים למדות. כי לא בכל המקומות יהיו שוים מדות היין והחטה, אבל במקום אשר הם קונים הם יותר גדולות ובמקום אשר הם מוכרים יותר קטנות. וכן המשפטים אשר אינם טבעיים כי הם אנושיים, אינם אחדים בכל מקום כי גם לא ישוב המדינה.[13] אבל א' בכל מקום לבד משובח כפי הטבע. אמנם כל א' מהדברים המשובחים מהמשפט והדת, הם כן כמו הכללים אם הפרטים, כי הדברים הנפעלים הם רבים, ובכל א' מהם הוא אחד והנה הוא כולל.

    (commonly accepted). It is plausible that both factors combined led Baruch to select the term מפורסמים in this context.

12 This significant addition may have its origins in the Latin translation of Bruni ("non est quidem"), but it is a fairly liberal translation of it. The first Latin translation renders "qui quidem omne" without the negative element, whereas Rabbi Alguadez does not translate these words at all in his translation.

13 Here there is also a clear influence from Rabbi Alguadez's translation. Bruni's Latin translation renders it as "lege providentur".

CHAPTERS 1-3: SUMMARY

In sum, it becomes evident that the various medieval translations render Aristotle's text in distinct ways. The first translation, the Arabic one, diverges significantly from the Greek original. The Arabic translator makes an effort to present Aristotle's position as more coherent than in the Greek original, with the opinion of Aristotle tending more toward relative morality in the Arabic text than in the original.

Conversely, the first Latin translation tends in the opposite direction, subtly aligning the text of the *Ethics* with the concept of natural law. However, its Hebrew translation by Rabbi Alguadez diverges from its source, returning the text to a more relativistic interpretation.

The second Latin translation, by Bruni, is probably the closest to the Greek original, as Bruni appears to recognize the philosophical significance of the alterations made by the earlier Latin translation and endeavours to "correct" them. Similarly, the second Hebrew translation by Rabbi Baruch closely adheres to the Greek original, likely due to his use of Bruni's translation as a corrective reference. Nevertheless, there is still some influence from the first Hebrew translation on the second, causing this translation to lean slightly toward a relativistic interpretation of the *Ethics*, departing slightly from the original Greek text.

Two distinct "ethics of translation" seem to emerge from our analysis. Ishaq b. Hunain and Rabbi Alguadez appear to recognize the inherent tension within Aristotle's text. They endeavor to render the text more coherent, possibly reflecting a clear relativistic viewpoint. Consequently, their translations of the *Ethics* exhibit a distinct leaning toward relativism, with Ishaq taking a more pronounced stance in this direction than Rabbi Alguadez.

Conversely, Bruni and Rabbi Baruch seem to perceive the primary objective of the translator as approximating the Greek original as closely as possible, preserving its internal tensions and contradictions. The Latin translation by Grosseteste and Moerbeke adopts a middle-ground approach, introducing some alterations, albeit in a subtle manner that does not entirely resolve the internal tensions and contradictions of the Greek text. This approach, in turn, allows Rabbi Alguadez to offer a contrasting translation into Hebrew.

In the subsequent chapter, we will scrutinize the *Compendium* authored by Averroes. This text can be regarded as a form of paraphrase that occupies an intermediary position between a direct translation and a commentary.

CHAPTER FOUR: AVERROES' *COMPENDIUM* (MIDDLE COMMENTARY)

Averroes (1126-1198) was one of the most important Muslim philosophers of the Middle Ages. A portion of his writings relate his personal philosophical views (such as the *Incoherence of the Incoherence* against Al-Ghazali). However, he achieved his greatest influence through his various commentaries on Aristotle. Averroes himself categorized these commentaries according to length, using terms that have been standardly translated as "Short", "Middle", and "Long".[1] Some of the Jewish and Latin philosophers did not use a full translation of the works of Aristotle, but only the short and middle commentaries of Averroes.[2] On the *Nicomachean Ethics*, Averroes composed only a middle commentary. Though the original Arabic text of Averroes is no longer extant,[3] both a Hebrew and a Latin translation survive. The Latin

---

[1] The short commentaries are summaries of Aristotle's writings; the middle commentaries' paraphrase entire texts of Aristotle; whilst the long commentaries are detailed, line-by-line analyses that also cite many other philosophers as well as earlier commentaries on Aristotle.

[2] On the Averroistic trend in Jewish and Christian philosophy, see Renan 1925; Hayoun 1991.

[3] On this subject, see Berman 1967; however, note that in this article there are no excerpts from the seventh chapter of the fifth book, which we have been analysing.

translation was carried out by Hermannus Alemannus around the middle of the thirteenth century, probably in Spain.[4] The Hebrew translation was executed by Samuel B. Yehuda of Marseille and published in three different versions over the years 1320-1322.[5]

In this chapter, we will compare Averroes' commentary, or more accurately, its Hebrew and Latin translations, with the original Greek text, as well as with the Arabic and Latin translation of Aristotle. At the end of the chapter, we provide comprehensive quotations from both the Latin and Hebrew translations of Averroes. Additionally, we will examine certain discrepancies between the Hebrew and Latin translations of Averroes' works.

With all of the above noted, we may identify six key differences between Averroes and the direct translations from the Greek; in the text included at the end of this chapter, we will emphasize the major changes he effected.

1. *Non-natural justice is considered positive and dependent on the particularities of each nation.*

The first difference is in the beginning of the chapter, where Averroes defines all justice as conventional (נימוסי in the Hebrew translation). In order to make a distinction between the conventional justice implied by the original Greek and the natural one, Averroes has to add that non-natural justice is positive or instructional (positivum/הנחיי). He also adds that this positive justice is

---

[4] I have consulted, for this text, the Venice 1483 edition.

[5] For more information on the Hebrew translation, see Berman 1967, pp. 11-51.

dependent on the particular nation (secundum diversas gentes/כפי אומה ואומה). The original Greek and its various translations speak only in the beginning of the chapter of changes in place, time, and the thinking of the people. These changes are in and of themselves not especially significant. However, they make the difference between natural and legal law sharper, and this clarity has significance further on in the text.[6]

2. Conventional classes are natural.

A significant departure in Averroes' *Compendium* from the Greek original arises within the realm of conventional justice. Averroes' text introduces a distinction between the categories (genere/סוג) of conventional matters and the more specific (commensuratione/הנחי) ones. The categories, or classes, of conventional matters are, in fact, considered natural. Conversely, the specific laws are entirely conventional. This differentiation becomes apparent in the examples mentioned by Aristotle. Sacrifice and ransom for prisoners, for instance, possess a natural quality that transcends time and place, but their precise quantities are subject to convention and vary across different regions and eras. However, this specific differentiation between the classes and specifics of conventional law does not exist in the original Greek text. This disparity holds significance as it presents an alternative viewpoint: solely the specific conventional laws

---

[6] A difference between the Hebrew and the Latin text of Averroes is that the Hebrew translates justice (عدل in Arabic) by the word שווי (balance). This translation aligns the theory of justice with the doctrine of the mean more than any other translation or commentary.

are genuinely conventional, while their classes retain a natural essence. Indeed, the inclusion of this additional distinction, coupled with Cicero's influence on the Latin commentator, has a profound impact on the perspective of Thomas Aquinas. Consequently, this viewpoint reverberates among later Latin commentators. We can also discern this very same perspective emerging in certain Jewish commentators who have been influenced by Averroes and/or Thomas Aquinas.

3. *Omission of the passage on the gods.*

The second important change is the omitting of the passage on the gods in Averroes' version. This change is very significant because that sentence was a major justification for the total rejection (as in the Arabic translation) or acceptance (as in the Greek original and Latin translation) of natural law. By the omission of this sentence, Averroes makes a clear difference between natural and conventional law, with natural law very much applying to human affairs in as real a way as conventional law. As we saw earlier, the Greek original and its Latin translation use the point of view of the gods to explore the possibility of a complete negation of entirely conventional law and the concomitant limitation on all legal differences regarding human opinion. By contrast, the Arabic version opens the possibility of the complete rejection of natural law by creating an option that natural law exists only in the human sphere.

4. *Some natural laws are as inherent as the burning of fire.*

Averroes introduces a significant alteration to the example of fire. In the Greek original and the known Arabic translations, the argument of those who deny the existence of natural law is grounded in the assumption that every natural law must possess the same consistency and universality as the phenomenon of fire. According to the original Greek, Aristotle agrees that there is no law that is natural in the same sense as the burning of fire. People who define law as natural only if the naturalness is like the burning of fire conclude that there is no such thing as natural law. By contrast, in Averroes' commentary, the text posits that there are some natural laws that are as natural as fire, i.e. laws that are exactly the same in all places and times. This key difference also creates a sharp distinction between natural and specific conventional laws.[7]

V. Omission of the words "that both are equally changeable".

Averroes also omits the words "that both are equally changeable" (ἄμφω κινητὰ ὁμοίως [يتحرك كلاهما in the Arabic]),[8] which the reader will recall can refer either to natural and conventional law, or else to changes that can be natural or conventional. This elision further sharpens the distinction between natural and specific conventional

---

[7] Regarding this matter, Averroes' Latin translation includes a phrase absent from the Hebrew translation: "Ex rebus igitur iustis secundum hoc quaedam erunt effectivae iusti ex parte naturae." In my assessment, this alteration does not introduce a significant philosophical shift. It primarily serves to emphasize that natural justice remains consistent across all circumstances, as it does not vary with time or customs. We have marked this addition in the text given at the end of the chapter.

[8] For the same reason, as mentioned in the previous footnote, we cannot mark this omission in the Latin appendices.

law because in place of these words, Averroes uses language that underscores that only conventional laws can change, while natural law by definition never changes. By contrast, in the Greek original, the passage concerning the mutability of both natural and conventional law was one of the major elements of the chapter moderating the difference between the two kinds of law. It was on this very point that the Arabic translation has Aristotle unequivocally asserting that natural law never changes and remains exactly the same in all places, while conventional law is completely relative to place and time, such that in the human realm, only conventional law can apply since any potential natural law must bend to the vicissitudes of human existence and circumstances.

It is important to note that Averroes' commentary is nearer to the Greek text at this point than to the Arabic translation vis-á-vis the apparent stand of the Greek on absolute natural law.[9] The most probable explanation for this fact is that Averroes decided to continue with the sharp distinction between natural and conventional law, which are also mentioned in the beginning of the Arabic translation, though in the latter parts of the Arabic translation this distinction becomes muted by the need to have natural law conform to circumstances. This decision, which differs from the understanding (or the decision) of the Arabic translator, makes his text nearer to the Greek than to the Arabic translation. Another possibility is that Averroes somehow was familiar with the original Greek

---

[9] Especially regarding the third difference between the original Greek and the Arabic translation, i.e. the omission of hard natural law existing only amongst the gods.

text. A third possibility to consider is that Averroes relied on a second Arabic translation, which is now lost.

Exploring this possibility would be particularly intriguing, as it could potentially reveal divergences between the two Arabic translators who shaped the reception of Aristotle's ethical views in distinct trajectories. It is also possible that the Latin and Hebrew translators changed the text of Averroes due to their knowledge of the Greek text or its Latin translation.[10] Another plausible option is that Averroes may have been influenced by the same ancient Latin sources that exerted an impact on the medieval Latin commentators, particularly figures such as Cicero. While this influence may appear less likely, it still remains a possibility that certainly warrants further investigation. Exploring the potential influence of the Roman philosopher on Averroes adds an intriguing dimension to the study of their relationship. To decide this question, we would need to make a more thorough analysis of all the commentaries of Averroes, as well as the Arabic translation in other subjects.

VI. Omission of the fluctuating price example.

Another change is the omission by Averroes of the concluding part of the example of fluctuating prices in different markets, which follows the example of acquired

---

[10] This last possibility may seem less probable because the Hebrew and Latin translations of Averroes are in accord with one another and thus we do not see any room to argue that the Hebrew translator was influenced by the Latin version of Averroes' *Middle Commentary*.

ambidexterity.[11] In the Greek original (and in the Arabic translation), Aristotle said that measures differ in different places. However, there is something that remains the same in all places, namely that measures are "larger in wholesale and smaller in retail markets" (ὠνοῦνται, μείζω, οὗ δὲ πωλοῦσιν, ἐλάττω / التي يشترى بها أكبر والتي يباع بها أصغر). Averroes entirely omits this part of the sentence. This change is noteworthy because the Greek here maintains that there is something unchangeable and natural at the root of all changes in conventional laws. The text of Averroes, by contrast, has this example positing that in the sphere of specific legal changes there is no place for natural law.

7. *Change to the last sentence to sharpen the distinction between natural and conventional law.*

The last major difference we will examine relates to the controversial sentence about the ideal conventional law or urbanity. In the Greek original (and its Latin and Arabic translations),[12] we saw that it is possible to understand this sentence in two different and actually opposite ways: either that there is one natural law that is the best in all places, or there is one natural law in each place that changes according to the place and time. In both alternatives, Aristotle speaks on the relationship of the system of government to natural law. The text of Averroes relates this passage in a completely different way. Because

---

[11] In the example of acquired ambidexterity, Averroes also makes a minor change when he explains that the left hand can become a kind of right hand in the case of a man who becomes ambidextrous.

[12] Which we saw in the preceding part of the article.

of the importance of this sentence, I provide here the Hebrew and the Latin versions, followed by a single English translation since they are to all respects and purposes identical:

Et hoc quoniam quemadmodum leges et modi vivendi non sunt uni in omni loco. Sic se habet in rebus iustis. Et est quidem modus vivendi naturalis unus in omni loco. Positivus autem non est unus in omni loco.	וזה כי כמו שהתורות וההנהגות אינם אחדות בכל מקום כן הענין בדברים השווים. ואמנם תהיה ההנהגה אחת בכל מקום ההנהגות הטבעיות ואולם ההנחיות הנה לא יהיו אחדות בכל מקום

And in the same way the laws and the modes of life are not one in all places, so it is regarding matters of justice. Indeed, the mode of life that is one in all places is the natural mode of life. Directives [i.e., conventional laws], nevertheless, are not one in all places.[13]

The text of Averroes is completely different from both the original and its different translations. In this passage, Averroes summarizes the opinion that he expounds on throughout the passage: that there is a clear difference between the conventional part (positivus / ההנחיות) of the law which changes in relation to place and time, and the natural part of the law that is the same in every place and time.[14] Instead of explaining the relationship between conventional law and nature, Averroes accentuates the sharp difference between them. Averroes returns by the

---

[13] This translation is mine (with thanks to Robert Klein).

[14] As with the Arabic translation, the term "the best" (ἡ ἀρίστη) does not exist in the text of Averroes.

end of the text to the sharp differences between natural law, which is uncompromisingly stable, and specific conventional law, which always changes in relation to time and place.

In summary, we can observe significant divergence between Averroes' text and the Greek original, as well as the Arabic and Latin translations. Averroes presents a more coherent explanation of our chapter compared to the Greek original and other medieval translations. A key distinction made by Averroes is the differentiation between natural law, which remains constant irrespective of place and time, and conventional law, which can be further subdivided into specific laws that vary according to place, time, custom, or legislation, and unchangeable categories similar to natural law. In the original Aristotle, there are passages that contradict this sharp division. These passages suggest that there is no natural law in the sense of the nature of fire, and instead, all things are subject to change, although there is something natural in all conventional matters and vice versa. Averroes eliminates, modifies, or reinterprets these passages to create a more internally consistent text than the original. He removes sections of the Aristotelian text that could allow for changes in natural law. With this interpretation, Averroes establishes a distinct division between specific conventional and natural law that appears to deviate from Aristotle's more flexible approach to these questions.

It is important to note that Averroes also differs from the existing Arabic and Latin translations. The extant Arabic translation emphasizes a relativistic interpretation of the *Ethics*, while the Latin translation by Grosseteste, in contrast, introduces a (lesser) alteration in favour of a "natural law friendly" interpretation of the *Ethics*. Bruni's Latin translation aligns more closely with the original Greek and makes only minor changes in a similar manner to the previous Latin translation. In subsequent chapters, we will explore the significant influence of Averroes on Jewish and Latin commentators.

The Translations of Averroes

Because the commentary of Averroes is not a translation, but more of paraphrase of Aristotle's text, the cutting up of the chapter into three passages does not correspond exactly to the division that we saw in the original Greek and its Arabic and Latin translations.

Translation of Averroes in Latin[15]	*Translation of Averroes in Hebrew*[16]

I.

Iustitiae autem civilis quiddam est naturale legale et quiddam legale tantum, <u>id est positivum.</u> Ius autem naturale est, cuius mensura est in omni loco et in omni tempore et non cadit in ipsum commensuratio. Lex autem non naturalis <u>genere</u> quidem quasi naturalis est et non est	אמר השווי המדיני קצתו טבעי נימוסי וקצתו נימוסי לבד ר״ל הנחי. ואולם השווי הטבעי הנה הוא שווי אשר כוחו אחד בכל מקום ובכל זמן ולא תפול בו תמורה. ואולם הנימוסי אשר אינו טבעי הנה הוא אם <u>בסוג הוא</u> כאלו הוא טבעי ואין בו חלוף ואם

---

[15] *Commentum Averrois super libros Ethicorum ad Nicomachum Aristotelis*, ed. Carsten Schliwski and Raphaela Veit (Cologne, 2011). A product of the Digital Averroes Research Environment, Thomas-Institute, University of Cologne, the text of this digital edition is based on Munich, Bayerische Staatsbibliothek Ink A 701, an exemplar of the *editio princeps* of Aristotle's works: Aristoteles, *Opera*, Pars III.2: *Ethica ad Nicomachum, Politica, Oeconomica*, ed. Nicoletus Vernia (Venice: Andreas Torresanus and Bartholomaeus de Blavis, 1483), foll. 27r-68r.

[16] Based on Berman's edition, pp.189-190.

in ea diversitas. Commensuratione autem diversificatur <u>secundum diversas gentes</u>, ut iustitia posita commensurativae in decollocutionibus et oblationibus et orationibus positis in legibus et foris.

<u>בשעירה הוא מתחלף באומה
אומה</u> כמו השווי המונח בשעירת הזבחים והקרבנות המונחות בדתות ובתורות.

II.

Dixit: Et quidam hominum vident quod omnes iustitiae legales positivae sunt in quibus incidit commensuratio et variatio secundum quod videtur unicuique ex legum latoribus, quod sit convenientius variare secundum locum et tempus. Quae vero sunt per naturam non diversantur quando sit vis eius una in omni loco et in omni tempore, <u>sicut ignis vis una est in omni loco, intendo quod ipse movetur sursum ubicumque ponatur in mundo et quacumque hora ponatur. Ex rebus igitur iustis secundum hoc quaedam erunt effectivae iusti ex parte naturae.</u>

אמר וקצת האנשים יסברו שכל השווים הנימוסיים ההנחיים יפול בם התמורה והשינוי כפי שיראה מניח מניח ממניחי הנימוסים להיות היותר נאות בם מתחלף כפי המקום והזמן. ואולם אשר הם בטבע הנה לא יתחלפו אחר שהיה כחם אחד בכל מקום וזמן <u>כמו האש אשר כוחה אחד בכל מקום, רצוני שהיא תתנועע אל מעלה באי זו פאה הונחה מן העולם ובאי זו עת הונחה</u>.

III.

Et quaedam effectivae ex parte consuetudinis non ex parte naturae suae per suam qualitatem, sed ex parte positionis et usus earum. Et quemad-

הנה יהיו הדברים השווים כפי זה מהם פועלים לשווי מפני הטבע ומהם פועלים מפני המנהג לא מפני טבעיהם

modum dextra manus est dextra naturaliter et sinistra interdum fit dextra usualiter, sic est dispositio in iustitiis naturalibus et consuetudinibus. Et commensuratio diversificata secundum magis et minus secundum quamlibet legem *in istis iustitiis diversis per legem*, intendo media, quae sunt in ipsis. Et si sint multae et diversae secundum diversas gentes sunt tamen omnes convenientes in hoc, quod faciunt factum iustitiae et quasi in hoc similatur mensuris diversis, quibus utuntur in qualibet civitate. Ipse etenim et si sint diversae omne tamen faciunt factum iustitiae, intendo mensuras tritici et olei et consimilium, quae mensurantur. Nam non sunt istae mensurae quantitas unius apud omnes gentes. Sic igitur est dispositio rerum iustarum quodammodo. Et istud est, ut commensuratio orationum et servitiorum in qualibet lege. Et hoc quoniam quemadmodum leges et modi vivendi non sunt uni in omni loco. Sic se habet in rebus iustis. Et est quidem modus vivendi naturalis unus in omni loco. Positivus autem non est unus in omni loco.

באיכותם אבל מפני ההנחה והעשיה להם. וכמו שהיד הימנית היא ימנית בטבע והשמאלית כבר תהיה ימנית בהרגל כן העניין בשווים הטבעיים וההרגליים. והשעירה מתחלפת בפחות והיתר כפי נימוס נימוס באלו השווים המתחלפים בנימוס, רצוני האמצעיים אשר בם, ואם היו רבים מתחלפים כפי *אומה אומה* הנה הם כלם יתקבצו כשהם יפעלו פועל השווי. וכאלו הם בזה יתדמו המשורות המתחלפות אשר יעשו במדינה מדינה. הנה הם ואם היו מתחלפות הנה הם כלם יפעלו פועל השווי, רצוני מדת החטה והשמן וזולת זה ממה שימדד. כי אין המדה בעלת שעור אחד אצל כל האומות וכן הוא העניין בדברים השווים בפנים מה. וזה הוא כמו שעירת התפלות והעבודות בדת דת. וזה כי כמו שהתורות וההנהגות אינם אחדות בכל מקום כן העניין בדברים השווים. ואמנם תהיה ההנהגה אחת בכל מקום ההנהגות הטבעיות ואולם ההנחיות הנה לא יהיו אחדות בכל מקום.

SECTION TWO

MEDIEVAL COMMENTARIES

CHAPTER FIVE: GREEK BYZANTINE COMMENTATORS

In this chapter, we will undertake an analysis of three Byzantine commentators who have provided their insights on the seventh chapter of the fifth book of Aristotle's *Ethics*.[1] These commentaries date from the twelfth to the early fourteenth century and offer valuable perspectives on the Byzantine understanding of this chapter of the *Nicomachean Ethics* within the context of Byzantine culture. It is important to note that the Byzantines were the sole medieval thinkers with direct access to Aristotle's original texts, as they did not rely on translations. Consequently, they hold a significant position in the narrative of the reception of Aristotelian ethics during the medieval period.

---

[1] The remaining Greek commentator does not provide a commentary on the *Ethics*. For further information on Greek Byzantine commentators, one may refer to the collected essays in Barber and Jenkins 2009. Additionally, matter about Georgios Pachymeres' commentary on the *Nicomachean Ethics* can be found in Xenophontos 2022, pp. XXI-XXIII. It is important to note that there are no surviving ancient Greek commentaries on the *Ethics*. Although Alexander of Aphrodisias, Simplicus, Ammonius, Philoponus, and Themistius have written on ethical matters, none of their works should be considered commentaries on the *Ethics*. As for the commentary of Aspasius on the *Ethics*, the extant version does not include book V, but rather covers books 1-4 and 7-8.

The first commentator to be examined is the Anonymous (likely early twelfth century),[2] followed by Michael of Ephes (mid-twelfth century) as the second commentator,[3] and finally, Georgios Pachymeres (from 1242 to 1310) as the third.[4] Through an examination of their works, we shall observe that these three commentators offer a distinctive type of philosophical interpretation that significantly diverges from the perspectives of Averroes, the Arabic translation, and the Latin commentators.

The Byzantine commentators follow Aristotle's text closely and emphasize the distinctions between natural law, which is universally applicable, and conventional law, which is subject to change. In their interpretation, they do not fully align with the views of the Latin commentators, who strongly advocate for natural law, nor with the relativist approach found in the Arabic translation. The first two commentators assert that certain individuals cannot adhere to natural law due to inherent natural inferiority. However, Georgios presents a more relativistic viewpoint by omitting this addition and interpreting the end of the text as entirely relativistic.

The anonymous commentator

The anonymous Greek commentator, who was from the Byzantine era, likely early twelfth century, had his work

---

[2] The Greek text of the commentary is available in *Eustratii et Michaelis et anonyma, In Ethica Nicomachea commentaria*, Gustav Heylbut (ed.), first published Berlin, De Gruyter, 1892.

[3] *Michaelis Ephesii in librum quintum Ethicorum Nicomacheorum commentarium*, Berlin, De Gruyter, 1901.

[4] On this commentator see Xenophontos 2022.

translated into Latin by Robert Grosseteste during the time of his translation of the *Ethics*. Notably, Grosseteste translated parts from three different Greek commentaries, with the anonymous commentator's work specifically applied to the fifth book. However, upon examination, it becomes evident that this commentator's interpretation of Aristotle differs significantly from the Latin tradition and likely had minimal influence on the way medieval Latin Christians interpreted the concept of natural law.

Similar to other commentaries, the anonymous Greek commentator endeavours to establish greater coherence in Aristotle's ideas compared to the original text. However, this is done from a distinct perspective. In summary, this commentator presents a complex interpretation of the chapter, distinguishing between a general natural law, which represents the best course naturally, and the particular nature of different peoples, times, and places. These variations may deviate from the objective and genuine natural law. Individuals who are unprepared for the authentic natural law are deemed inferior in their nature compared to those who can live in accordance with it, as it represents the optimal path for human nature and society.

I.

At the outset of the first passage, it becomes apparent that the anonymous commentator imposes limitations on the definition of natural justice (and natural law). In accordance with his interpretation, the words of Aristotle, "φυσικὸν μὲν τὸ πανταχοῦ τὴν αὐτὴν ἔχον δύναμιν" ("natural, that which everywhere has the same force"), are construed as applicable to the majority of places and times. The commentator introduces additional words to augment Aristotle's original statement:

πανταχου δέ φησιν αντί του παρια τοίς πλείστοι. εισι γάρ τινα εθνη α ού χατα τουτο νομίζει. εν γαρ τοίς αδιαστρόφως χαί χατα φύσιν εχουσι. χαι δια τουτο τοίς πλείστοις οσιόν έστι το θεους σέβειν, γονείς τιμαν, πλανωμένοις, όδον επιδειχνύειν.	However, he claims that "everywhere" means "according to the majority." For there are some nations that do not consider this. They have it based on what is immutable and according to nature. And for this reason, it is holy for the majority to worship the gods, honor their parents, and show the way to the wanderers.

According to the anonymous commentator, the term *everywhere* (πανταχου) does not encompass all places and times, but rather denotes the majority of them. In the subsequent statement, the commentator acknowledges that the natural law of the majority is inherently superior to the less optimal nature of the minority (εν γαρ τοίς αδιαστρόφως χαί χατα φύσιν εχουσι). The unchanging nature of justice is embraced by the majority, for whom it is naturally preferable to revere God, honour their parents, and guide those who are lost. However, for a minority of individuals (and potentially specific times and places), it is unnatural to accept these laws. Their nature is better suited to not conform to these laws or customs. This discrepancy may stem from their inferior nature, rendering them incapable of adhering to laws that align with the true nature of humanity and society.

At the onset of this commentary, it becomes evident that there is a notion of a natural law that possesses an objective superiority. However, this law does not align with the nature of all individuals, as well as various times and places. The anonymous commentator strives to establish coherence within this chapter of Aristotle by introducing a distinction between two types of natures. One is an unchanging nature that represents the optimal path for all peoples, while the other is a specific nature attributed to each distinct group and geographical location.

In contrast to these two forms of natural law, there are also conventional laws that entirely rely on the decisions of legislators or the prevailing customs of a particular place. These laws do not differ in terms of quality; rather, different peoples may have different laws that are considered equal, solely dependent on variations in their respective locations and historical periods.

Towards the conclusion of the first passage, the anonymous commentator provides historical context by referencing the exemples offered by Aristotle.

II.

In the second passage, the anonymous commentator maintains a consistent approach to his explanation. Initially, he remains faithful to Aristotle and clarifies that, contrary to the beliefs of certain individuals, not all laws are conventional. There exist laws that are inherent to human nature and can be considered natural.

As the passage draws to a close, the commentator reiterates his definition of natural law once again:

πως γαρ αχίνητα τα φύσει, ούχ άπλως. τη γάρ αύτων φύσει αχίνητα, ει χαί μη	For how are things unchangeable according to nature? Not universally. For

παρα τοίς χρωμένοι αύτοίς. αμα δε δια τούτων γνώριμον εσται ειπων χαί το πως ειπε φυσιχον είναι το πανταχου την αύτην δύναμιν εχον. εστι γαρ ώς τό φύσει δίκαιον χαί παρα πασίν έστι τοιουτον. παρα γαρ τοίς χατά φύσιν εχουσιν. ούχ άπλως παρά πασιν, ωσπερ το πυρ χαυστιχον χαι το τή αύτου φύσει αγαθον αγαθόν έστιν ώς πάντας ωφελείν τους χατά φύσιν εχοντας, άλλ ούχ άπλως πάντας, χαί το χατά φύσιν γλυχυ γλυχάζον έστlν ώς πάντας γλυχάζειν τους ύγιεινοντας.	they are unchangeable by their own nature, except when they are influenced by those who use them. But if someone is familiar with these things and can explain how it is said that everywhere it has the same power, for it is said that justice is according to nature and is the same for all, as it is according to those who have it in accordance with nature, not universally, but according to those who have it naturally. Not universally, like fire, which is useful and good by its own nature, as it benefits all those who have it according to nature, but not universally, but it is sweet to those who have a sweet taste, as it makes all those who are healthy happy.

At the beginning of the quoted text, the anonymous commentator provides an explanation that highlights the immutable nature of natural justice and laws, but emphasizes that they are not universally applicable. Drawing from the example presented at the end of this passage, and consistent with the rest of the commentary, natural justice exists in all places but is influenced by the individuals who engage in the pursuit of justice. The anonymous commentator offers a compelling illustration to reinforce this point. He likens justice to something akin to sweetness, which is inherently good by nature, but only brings happiness to those who are in good health. There are individuals for whom sweetness does not bring joy, because they are not in good health. Similarly, the same principle applies to natural justice. For those with a virtuous and superior nature, natural justice represents the pinnacle of righteousness. However, for individuals with an inferior nature, they are unable to uphold the unalterable principles of natural justice. It is incongruous with their inherently inferior disposition, much like how sick individuals do not derive pleasure from consuming sweet foods.

III.

In the third passage, the anonymous commentator maintains his philosophical stance, delving deeper into his perspective. Initially he explains, closely aligned with Aristotle's original text, that natural law can indeed undergo change. Continuing his discourse, he proceeds to elucidate the example of the right hand, illustrating his philosophical viewpoint:

ουτω γαρ λέγομεν χαι την δεξιαν χείρα φύσει χρειττονα χαι εχυρωτεραν ειναι, οτι επι των χατα' φυσιν εχοντων ουτως εχει. ουτω γαρ χαί φύσει δίπους άνθρωπος χαι φύσει δύο οφθαλμους εχει, χαίτοι ένδέχεται χαί ταίς χερσίν άμφοτέραις ισον τινα ισχύειν ώς τον Άστεροπαίον [οτι] χαί τή άριστερα πλέον χαί ενα	For this reason, we say that the right hand is by nature more necessary and stronger, as it is so with those who have it naturally. Likewise, a human by nature has two eyes and, although it is possible for both hands to have equal strength, it is more effective to have the right hand (stronger), just as having one foot or one eye is worse (than having two).

πόδα η ενα ωφθαλμον
εχειν.

According to the anonymous commentator, the ideal situation is for the right hand to be stronger than the left, surpassing even the ambidextrous condition.[5] This optimal scenario aligns with the natural order of things, much like individuals who can abide by natural laws. However, the commentator acknowledges that there are individuals who possess only one eye or one leg, rendering them incapable of the same actions as those who are healthy and possess two eyes and two legs. The anonymous commentator is the first to perceive the ambidextrous individual as being in a more disadvantageous situation than those who prefer to use their right hand. This elucidation lends support to the perspective that there exists a universal natural law applicable to all individuals, a notion that will become more pronounced in subsequent interpretations.

Furthermore, the commentator expounds upon their viewpoint by asserting that wealth is beneficial only for those who possess an inherent disposition towards wealth. For others, wealth can be detrimental. This highlights the notion that what is deemed best according to nature may not necessarily be favourable for the majority, but rather applicable to a minority who possess the capability to attain the natural good, as exemplified by wealth in this context.

---

[5] In conclusion, as we reach the end of the passage, it becomes evident that while there are some ambidextrous individuals who find themselves in a more advantageous position, they constitute a minority within the larger context.

Towards the end of the passage, the anonymous commentator interprets Aristotle's perplexing phrase, ἀλλὰ μία μόνον πανταχοῦ κατὰ φύσιν ἡ ἀρίστη (though there is but one (constitution) which is everywhere by nature the best), providing an additional insight into this passage:

ου γάρ πανταχου χαι παρά πασιν ή αύτη πολιτεία, ούδε παρα τοίς αυτοίς ή αυτη αιει, οτι μη φύσει αιεί άλλα νόμω τε χαί χατα συνθήχην συνίσταντα χαί τοιούτοις χρωνται διχαίοις. ή μέντοι άρίστη αιεί χαί παρα πασι τοίς χατα φύσιν εχουσιν ή αυτή. φύσει γαρ αυτη. χαι γαρ ει μη χατ' αυτα πολιτεύονται αλλα χατά φύσιν τέ έστιν αύτοίς ώς χαι το την δεξιάν χείρα εχειν χρειττω τοίς εχουσιν. αυτη δ' αν ειη έν η τά φυσιχα διχαια χαί νόμιμά έστι.

nor does it remain the same for all time in the same city, because it is not inherently the same but changes according to nature and conventions, and they use both justly. However, the best and always esteemed by all is what is in accordance with nature itself. For it is itself by nature, and if they do not govern according to it but against nature, it is to their detriment, just as those who have the right hand unnecessary [people who do not predominantly employ their right hand, even when their right hand is stronger]. And this should be in one, that the natural and the legal are the same.

In this text the anonymous commentator affirms that the law must change according to the nature of each people and society (or constitution). The constitution is the best in each place according to the nature of this specific place, people, and time. However, the people that cannot reach the true natural law by nature are like the people that have their right hand unnecessary (because there are ambidextrous). There are two kinds of natural law (or justice): the law that is natural for each people and time, and the law that is natural for all people (and times and places). The first emphasizes the relative nature of every society and the second the objective quality of all laws and societies according to their differences – we can compare the different quality of the societies by comparing the law that they can achieve. If they can reach the best natural law (i.e. the law that is the best according to human nature), they are the best, if not, they are of inferior quality.

The anonymous commentator does not interpret the example of the ambidexter as showing the amelioration of the natural situation by conventional law but as showing the fact that the common natural situation (that the right hand is stronger) is better than the exception.

To summarize, the anonymous Byzantine commentator holds the view that conventional laws are entirely equal across different societies; these laws may differ but possess equal standing. However, when it comes to the realm of natural justice or laws, the commentator introduces a distinction not present in Aristotle's original. This distinction is between the true natural law, which represents the best possible law, and the natural circumstances specific to each group of people and era. The commentator suggests that certain individuals are unable to attain the state that is naturally optimal for all humans and societies due to their inferior nature or development, although the reasons for this inferiority are not explicitly explained.

It is worth noting that the anonymous Greek commentator does not clearly differentiate between specific and general commandments. While the exemple demonstrates that natural law is more general, the commentator fails to clarify this distinction. In this regard, the commentator aligns with Aristotle and differs from the interpretations found in Averroes' *Compendium* and the Latin commentators, both of which have, in turn, influenced most Hebrew commentaries and translations.

Michael of Ephesus

Michael of Ephesus was a Byzantine commentator on Aristotle who lived during the mid-twelfth century. Upon examining his commentary, it becomes apparent that the anonymous commentator likely influenced Michael, as the main philosophical themes in their commentaries exhibit notable similarities. One significant indication of this probable influence is the shared usage of the same example (the sweet example in the second part of the passage), which suggests either a direct influence or the use of common sources.

In summarizing these commentaries, we find that they cover similar topics, but there are noteworthy differences as well. Particularly, Michael takes a more restricted approach to natural justice and law, focusing on a limited number of fundamental principles.

I.

In the initial section of the chapter, Michael aligns with the viewpoints of the anonymous commentator, affirming the existence of natural justice that is universally applicable across all locations. However, Michael acknowledges the presence of certain individuals who dwell in a state of savagery, devoid of any form of justice, be it conventional or natural:

τοίς θηριώδεσι χαι παντάπασι τον νοϋν έχτετυφλωμένοις και μόνην την ζωώδη διώχουσιν ηδονην ούχ εστι το Πολιτιχον διχαιον.	in relation to savage and irrational beings, who pursue only sensual pleasure, political justice does not exist.

In accordance with the viewpoints expressed by the anonymous commentator, Michael agrees that the observance of obligations towards gods and parents is an integral component of natural justice. However, he acknowledges that certain savage and irrational populations may fail to abide by this law. It is within this context that the inferior state of these savages is seen as a contributing factor to their non-compliance with the fundamental principles of natural law.

The primary divergence between these two commentators lies in the fact that Michael introduces an additional example pertaining to conventional law. He includes the instance of incestuous relationships as an illustration of a law that falls within the domain of conventional rather than natural law. By highlighting this example, Michael emphasizes that the scope of natural law, in his perspective, is limited to a select few basic principles, such as the reverence for parents and the worship of gods.

II.

In the second part of his commentary, Michael demonstrates a striking similarity to the anonymous commentator, strongly suggesting either direct influence or shared sources. He expounds upon the notion that individuals who fail to adhere to natural justice are of lesser moral standing compared to those who do. Drawing a parallel, he likens such individuals to those afflicted with physical ailments. Natural justice and its accompanying laws, he asserts, are universally applicable to all morally sound and upright individuals, as well as the gods. Only those individuals with an inherently inferior nature are unable to fully engage with and practice natural law. Michael employs the same example as the anonymous commentator—the analogy of sweet things being pleasing to individuals in good health. These sweet things possess an inherent goodness, irrespective of whether certain individuals, due to their inferior nature, reject or abstain from partaking in them.

III.

In the third part of his commentary, Michael raises a crucial question regarding the distinction between natural and conventional law in light of their propensity to change over time. He aligns his view with that of the anonymous commentator, claiming that natural laws, although universally the best, are subject to alteration due to certain individuals' inability to uphold them. To illustrate this point, he revisits the example of the right hand, interpreting the existence of ambidextrous individuals as being of lesser standing than those with a dominant right hand.

Where the two commentators diverge once again is in their delineation of the boundary between natural and conventional law. Michael specifically designates certain fundamental aspects, such as the type of government (aristocratic, democratic, or oligarchic), as components of conventional law. The anonymous commentator does not provide explicit clarity on this matter. According to Michael, only a select set of laws, including the reverence for parents and gods, fall within the purview of natural law. Conversely, any provisions pertaining to constitutional matters are susceptible to alterations that align with the transitions in the prevailing system of governance, characterized by their inherently conventional nature.

ὡς γαρ τά μετρα φησί προς το χρήσιμον αλλάττεται, ουτω χαι το χατά συνθήχην δίχαιον την αρχην μεν τιθεται δια το δοχείν συμφέρειν τω Χοινω, επειτα μεταπίπτει, ἡνίχα δοχεί μη συμφέρειν η οπου μη συμφέρει. ου γαρ το συμφέρον τη δημοχρατία συμφέρει Χαι τη ολιγαρχία η τη αριστοχρατία. ωστε επεί αλλο μεν το δίχαιον χαι το συμφέρον τη δημοκρατία, άλλο δε τη αριστοχρατία, ἐπειδαν ἡ πολιτεία οἷον ἡ δημοχρατία μεταπέση εις αριςτοχρατίαν η αυτη εις εχείνην δι' ας αιτίας λέγει ἐν ταις Πολιτείαις τας μεταπτώσεις αυτων γίνεσθαι, ανάγχη χαί τά νομιχά δίχαια μεταπίπτειν.	For, as it is said, the measures change with respect to their usefulness, and in this way what is conventionally just is initially established based on what is advantageous for the community, but then it changes when it is no longer advantageous. It is not in the interest of democracy or oligarchy or aristocracy. Therefore, since what is just and what is advantageous are different in democracy and aristocracy, when the form of government, such as democracy, changes to aristocracy or vice versa, due to the reasons (circumstances) of each states, the transitions occur necessarily, and the conventional justice changes.

οὒχ εισι δε πανταχου χαί παρα πασιν αἱ αυταί πολιτεία, διότι μη φύσει αλλά νομω χαί χατά συνθήχην συνίστανται χαί χρωνται χαί διχαίοις τοιούτοις. ἡ μέντοι αρίστη πολιτεία (ητις δέ έστιν αυτη, είρηχεν έν ταίς πολιτείαις) αεί χαί παρά πασιν τοίς χατα φύσιν εχουσιν ἡ αυτή έστι.	Moreover, constitutions are not the same everywhere and, in all cases, since they are not determined by nature but by law and convention, and they operate and function according to such conventions. However, the best constitution (which is itself, as it is said in the constitutions) always and in every case is the one that corresponds to what is naturally just.

According to Michael, the ideal constitution should align with the principles of natural law. However, he argues that natural law encompasses such minimal requirements that even aristocratic, democratic, and oligarchic constitutions can conform to it (although he does not explicitly mention tyrannical governments, which may lie outside the scope of natural law – presumably because the tyrannical government by definition do not rule in the interest of the community).

Additionally, Michael emphasizes that the definition of justice and law is contingent upon the specific form of constitution. For instance, in aristocratic and oligarchic systems, which discourage the participation of the majority in governance and emphasize a clear division between the elite and the general population, this division is regarded as just. On the other hand, in a democracy, such a distinction is considered unjust, as it privileges the wealthy and grants them greater influence over the government. By classifying the type of constitution as conventional rather than natural, Michael thereby highlights the significant role played by convention in shaping justice and law.⁶

In summary, Michael continues the philosophical trend set forth by the anonymous commentator, asserting that natural justice remains constant across all places and times. Both commentators agree that there exist individuals who do not adhere to natural justice due to their inherent inferiority, comparable to those lacking certain physical attributes or individuals who do not derive pleasure from sweet foods. However, a significant distinction between these Byzantine commentators emerges in Michael's provision of examples, which illustrate a significantly narrower scope for natural law. Specifically, Michael explicitly designates certain fundamental aspects of law, such as the type of constitution, as conventional. While the anonymous commentator does not clearly address this aspect, a careful reading of their works suggests a potentially broader conception of natural law compared to Michael.

Georgios Pachymeres

Georgios Pachymeres, a prominent historian and Byzantine philosopher who lived from 1242 to 1310, contributed significantly to the field with his commentary on Aristotle's *Ethics*. While his commentary is relatively concise, Pachymeres extensively quotes passages from Aristotle, augmenting them with his own inserted words and phrases. In the initial sections of his commentary, he

---

⁶ The subsequent section of Michael's commentary maintains a consistent philosophical trajectory.

adheres closely to the original text of Aristotle, expressing fewer philosophical opinions compared to the earlier Byzantine commentators.

However, a notable shift occurs in the third section of Pachymeres' commentary, where he introduces a significant alteration that aligns him more closely with relativism in contrast to the preceding Byzantine commentaries.

I.

In the first passage of his commentary, Georgios Pachymeres refrains from making any significant philosophical additions to Aristotle's words. Unlike the previous Byzantine commentators, he does not mention the existence of people who deviate from the principles of natural laws. Additionally, he does not assert, as his predecessors do, that those who cannot adhere to natural law are inherently inferior to others. These differences bring him closer to Aristotle's original text and also position him as more of a relativist compared to his predecessors.

In this passage, Georgios merely presents Aristotle's distinction between natural laws, which remain consistent everywhere, and conventional laws, which are contingent upon the decisions of legislators. The examples he adds to illustrate natural law — such as eating when hungry, honouring parents, avoiding suicide, and aiding those in need — are basic and do not introduce any substantial philosophical distinctions beyond what Aristotle had already articulated.

II.

Georgios provides a concise commentary on the second passage, offering insights into the perspectives of those who argue against the existence of universal natural laws. According to these individuals, natural law cannot be uniform across all places and times. They thereby reject its existence. Georgios also cites Aristotle, who acknowledges that this viewpoint is not entirely accurate, but only holds true to a certain extent. However, Georgios neglects to mention Aristotle's phrase regarding the gods' perspective, which staunchly opposes the relativist position and supports the notion of natural justice and law. This phrase represents a crucial passage that advocates for a universal natural law that remains consistent across all locations. Despite this omission, it does not significantly alter the original ideas presented by Aristotle.

III.

In the third passage, Georgios refrains from presenting a conclusive explanation regarding the comparative advantages or disadvantages of ambidexterity in relation to individuals with a dominant right hand. He presents the example of the ambidextrous individual to demonstrate that natural law, despite its inherent naturalness, can undergo changes akin to conventional law. However, the crucial modification in Georgios's argument occurs towards the conclusion of this passage. Here, Georgios asserts that the optimal law is not universally applicable across all times and locations but rather varies according to different constitutional arrangements, without explicitly referencing any natural foundation.

κατὰ φύσιν ἡ ἀρίστη.⁷ τῶν δὲ δικαίων καὶ νομίμων ἕκαστον ὡς τὸ καθόλου πρὸς τὰ καθέκαστα ἔχει· τὰ μὲν γὰρ πραττόμενα πολλὰ καὶ καθέκαστα, τὸ δὲ ἕν· καθόλου γάρ· δημοκρατία ἴσως ἢ ἀριστοκρατία ἢ βασιλεία· τούτων γὰρ ἕκαστον ἕν· καὶ τὸ μὲν δίκαιον ἑκάστης πολιτείας ἕν, πολλὰ δὲ κατ' αὐτὸ τὰ συμπίπτοντα.

That by nature, as it were, [is] the best. Each [type of] just and lawful [action] is related as a universal to the [corresponding] particulars; for the actions performed are many and particular, whereas each [type] is one, since it is universal; perhaps [it is] a democracy or an aristocracy or a monarchy; for each of these is one; and what is just for each political constitution is one, while the events included in it [i.e. the constitution and thus the area it governs] are many.

In this text, Georgios provides a more pronounced relativist interpretation of the passage from Aristotle compared to Michael, who also acknowledges the conventional nature of different constitutions while asserting that each constitution must adhere to a shared natural law. Georgios, on the other hand, posits that each constitution possesses its own inherent nature. However, there are no objective criteria grounded in nature to determine the superiority of one constitution over another. While the functioning of monarchy, aristocracy,

---

⁷ This marks the conclusion of the passage which I previously cited in the other commentaries and translations. Nevertheless, owing to the significance of this passage in comprehending the relationship between Georgios' and Michael's commentaries, I have chosen to include the subsequent two sentences in my citation of the text.

or democracy[8] necessitates a certain set of laws, the judgment regarding the most favorable constitution is entirely based on convention.

In summary, Georgios aligns with Aristotle's view in the first two passages, with only minor modifications that lean towards a relativist interpretation. However, in the third passage, his relativist stance becomes more pronounced compared to other Byzantine commentators. Similar to our previous commentator, Georgios acknowledges Aristotle's assertion that there exist two types of justice or law: 1. natural law, which remains consistent across all places and times, and 2. conventional law, which is subject to change. Like Michael, Georgios considers the question of constitution to be conventional and does not introduce any natural common ground in the final passage, in contrast to the anonymous commentator and Michael. Consequently, it can be concluded that Georgios' viewpoint aligns more closely with that of Michael, rather than the anonymous commentator. However, his commentary offers a significantly more relativist interpretation of Aristotle's text, particularly evident towards the end of the passage.

Conclusion

This chapter examines the viewpoints of three distinct Byzantine commentators on Aristotle. As we shall observe, similar to the Latin commentaries, a discernible

---

[8] It is noteworthy to acknowledge that Michael refers to oligarchy, while Georgios specifically addresses monarchy. Both commentators omit any reference to tyranny, yet they both make mention of democracy and aristocracy.

philosophical trend emerges among these commentators, which sets them apart from the trend found in the Latin commentaries. All Byzantine commentators embrace the division between natural law, which is objectively superior, and conventional law, which varies according to different peoples, places, and times, yet can still be equal while being different.

The anonymous commentator and Michael introduce a philosophical viewpoint that is not explicitly mentioned in Aristotle's text. According to this perspective, certain individuals are unable to attain the objective truth of natural law due to some form of inferiority. For these individuals, the true natural law is not the best choice because of their inferior nature. It is plausible to surmise that the anonymous commentator could argue in favor of democracy as the superior constitution, while some individuals perceive democracy as inferior due to their inferior nature or state of constitutional development.

Michael extends the opinion of the anonymous commentator on the main subject and was likely influenced by him. However, Michael limits natural justice (or law) to a few fundamental principles, such as respecting parents and honouring the gods, while explicitly asserting that the choice of constitution is entirely conventional.

Georgios, by contrast, does not mention the possibility of natural inferiority or individuals unable to practice natural justice (or law). Similar to Michael, he highlights the conventional nature of the constitution and dismisses its natural basis. These two additions make Georgios' commentary the most relativistic among the Byzantine commentators.

To conclude this chapter, we may observe that all Byzantine commentators adhere to a common interpretation of Aristotle that supports the existence of both natural and conventional law. However, significant differences exist among them, particularly between the anonymous commentator and Georgios, while Michael occupies an intermediate position. Michael aligns with the anonymous commentator regarding the notion of inferior natural circumstances and with Georgios when emphasizing the constitution as part of conventional law. The development of Byzantine perspectives on these subject warrants further investigation through extensive research focusing on diverse opinions within Byzantium concerning natural law.

Texts of the Byzantine commentators

In the following texts, quotation drawn from the original has been underlined.

The anonymous commentary.[9]

I.

<u>του δε πολιτιχου διχαου</u>. διαιρει το πολιτιχον δίχαιον εις το φυσιχον χαι νιομιχόν, όριζόμενος τί έχάτερον, χαί φησι το μεν <u>το πανταχου την αύτην εχον δύναμιν</u>. πανταχου δέ φησιν αντί του παρια τοίς πλείστοι. εισι γάρ τινα εθνη α ού χατα τουτο νομίζει. εν γαρ τοίς αδιαστρόφως χαί χατα φύσιν εχουσι. χαι δια τουτο τοίς πλείστοις οσιόν έστι το θεους σέβειν, γονείς τιμαν, πλανωμένοις, όδον επιδειχνύειν. πρόσκειται <u>καὶ οὐ τῷ δοκεῖν ἢ μή δια</u>[10] <u>νομικὸν</u> - ού γαρ τι δόξαι τισlν η μη το φυσιχον δίχαιον, αλλα το πολιτιχον. τουτο γαρ εξ αρχης μεν ουδεν διαφέρει, τεθέν δε χαl νομισθεν πολυ το διάφορον εχει, <u>οίον το μνας λυτρουσθαι.</u> τουτο γαρ 'Αθηναίοι χαι Λαχεδαιμόνιοι εν τω προς αλλήλους συνέθεντο πολέμω, το μνας λυτρουσθαι τους αιχμαλώτους. μνημονεύει της συνθήκης ταύτης 'Ανδροτίων. "Εὐχτήμων Κυδαθήναιος. έπι τούτου πρέσβεις ηλθον άπο Λαχεδαίμονος Άθήναζε Μέγιλλος χαί Ενδιος χαι Φιλοχαριδας" χαι επάγει "των δε περιγενομένων απεδοσαν μναν υπερ

---

[9] *Eustratii et Michaelis et anonyma In Ethica Nicomachea commentaria* edited by Gustav Heylbut, firstly published Berlin, De Gruyter, 1892, pp. 232-233.

[10] Δια is not in the original Greek that we have.

εκαστου λαβοντες". προειπων γαρ ην οτι τουτο συνέθεντο επί των άλισχομένων. ἢ τὸ αἶγα θύειν ἀλλὰ μὴ δύο πρόβατα, ουχ απο ιστοριας τινος εινρηται. το δε "Βρασίδα θύειν"[11]. Αμφιπολίται ποιουσιν, ώς ηρωϊ τούτω θύοντες.

II.

τό δε δοχεί δε ενίοις πάντα είναι τοιαυτα τοιουτόν εστιν. τινές εισι οι ούδεν οιονται φύσει δίχαιον είναι, αλλα πάντα θέσει τε χαι νόμω. χαί της δόξης την αιτιαν προσέθηχε. τουτο δε ούχ εστιν ούτως εχον αλλ' εστιν ως. τουτο δε ειρηχεν ητοι περὶ του δικαίου, οτι μη παν δίχαιον κινείται χαι ως τινες λεγουσιν (εστι γαρ ως το' διχαιον αχινητον χαι παρα τισι, παρα γαρ τοις χατα φύσιν εχουσιν), η προς το οτι το φύσει παν αχίνητον, ού γαρ εστι τούτο οϋτως έχον. πως γαρ αχίνητα τα φύσει, ούχ άπλως. τη γάρ αύτων φύσει αχίνητα, ει χαί μη παρα τοίς χρωμένοι αύτοίς. αμα δε δια τούτων γνώριμον εσται ειπων χαί το πως ειπε φυσιχον είναι το πανταχου την αύτην δύναμιν εχον. εστι γαρ ώς τό φύσει δίκαιον χαί παρα πασίν έστι τοιουτον. παρα γαρ τοίς χατά φύσιν εχουσιν. ούχ άπλως παρά πασιν, ωσπερ το πυρ χαυστιχον χαι το τή αύτου φύσει αγαθον αγαθον έστιν ώς πάντας ωφελείν τους χατά φύσιν εχοντας, άλλ ούχ άπλως πάντας, χαί το χατά φύσιν γλυχυ γλυχάζον έστὶν ώς πάντας γλυχάζειν τους ύγιεινοντας. το δε χαίτοι παρά γε τοῖς θεοῖς ἴσως ούδαμως εχον ειπεν ενδοξον· ει γαρ εστι τι παρα τοίς θεοίς δίχαιον, τουτο ουδέποτε

---

[11] In our Greek original "θύειν Βρασίδα".

μεταπίπτει ουδε ουδε άλλοις μεν αύτων έστι τοιουτον άλλοις δ' ου τω πάντας αύτους δμοίως εχειν.

III.

συγχωρων δε χαι το φύσει δίχαιον ειναι μεταχινητιχον χαὶ ένδεχόμενον χαι αλλως γίνεσθαι παρά τισιν ορίζεται αύτο τω τοίς χατα φύσιν εχουσι δοχείν τοιουτον. ουτω γαρ λέγομεν χαι την δεξιαν χείρα φύσει χρειττονα χαι εχυρωτεραν ειναι, οτι επι των χατα' φυσιν εχοντων ουτως εχει. ουτω γαρ χαί φύσει δίπους άνθρωπος χαι φύσει δύο οφθαλμους εχει, χαίτοι ένδέχεται χαί ταίς χερσίν άμφοτέραις ισον τινα ισχύειν ώς τον Άστεροπαίον [οτι] χαί τή άριστερα πλέον χαί ενα πόδα η ενα ωφθαλμον εχειν. χαί τα ψηφισμα τώδη, τα δια ψηφισμάτων χυρούμενα προς χαιρόν ,α όυχ ην διχαια πρίν τεθηναι, ώς το τας άρχας ώνητας ειναι άλλ' εστιν ως, τουτέστιν εστι τι χαι άχίνητον. χινητον μέντοι παν, διότι της του ένδεχομένου φύσεώς έστιν, ειπερ αμφω χινητα ομοίως. παρα γαρ τοίς άδιαστρόφως εχουσιν οντα ώς προείπεν ηδη. <u>χαίτοι ένδέχεται πάντας άμφιδεξίους γενέσθαι</u>· τουτο ουχ άργως προσέθηχεν, άλλ' ύπέρ του την χρίσιν ημας μη άπο του πλήθους άλλ άπο των χατα φύσιν έχόντων ποιείσθαι. ου γαρ οτι τοίς πλείστοις δ πλουτος χαχόν, διά τουτο ου τή φύσει αύτου άγαθόν, άλλα τοιουτος οτι τοίς χατα φύσιν εχουσιν αγαθόν. πως δε εχει το χατα συνθήχην δίχαιον, δ χαί συμφέρει, ειπέ τω δια το συμφέρειν δοχείν τω χοινω τίθεσθαί τε την άρχην χαί πάλιν μετατίθεσθαι <u>τοίς μέτροις</u> α προς το χρήσιμον άλλάσσεται, σαφως έπεδείξατο. <u>έπεί ουδε πολιτείας</u>. ου γάρ πανταχου χαι παρά πασιν ή αύτη πολιτεία, ούδε παρα τοίς αυτοίς ή αυτη αιει, οτι μη φύσει αιεί άλλα νόμφ τε χαί χατα συνθήχην συνίστανται χαί τοιούτοις χρωνται διχαίοις. ή μέντοι άρίστη αιεί χαί παρα πασι τοίς χατα φύσιν εχουσιν ή αυτή. φύσει γαρ αυτη. χαι γαρ ει μη χατ' αυτα πολιτεύονται αλλα χατά φύσιν τέ έστιν αύτοίς ώς χαι το την δεξιάν χείρα εχειν χρειττω τοίς εχουσιν. αυτη δ' αν ειη εν η τά φυσιχα διχαια χαί νόμιμά έστι.

Michael of Ephesus[12]

I.

τοϋ δε πολιτιχοϋ διχαίου το μεν φυσιχον το δε νομικόν, φυσιχον μεν το πανταχοϋ την αύτην εχον δύναμιν.

Τό πανταχού αντι τού παρά τοίς πλείστοις χαι αδιαστρόφοις και κατά φύσιν εχουσι. Παρά γάρ τοίς θηριώδεσι χαι παντάπασι τον νοϋν έχτετυφλωμένοις και μόνην την ζωώδη διώχουσιν ηδονην ούχ εστι το Πολιτιχον διχαιον. εστι δε χατα' φυσιν διχαον χαι εν τοις πλειστοις το σεβειν το θείον, το τιμαν τον πατέρα χαί την μητέρα, το έπαρχείν ενδεέσι, το τοίς πλανωμένοις την όδον επιδεικνύειν, τον εξ ολισθήματος πεπτωχότα έπανορθοϋν. είπων δε φυσιχον το <u>πανταχοϋ την αύτην εχον δύναμιν</u> έπήνεγχε <u>χαι ου τω δοχείν η μή</u>,

[12] *Michaelis Ephesii in librum quintum Ethicorum Nicomacheorum commentarium*, Berlin, De Gruyter, 1901, pp. 46-48.

χωρίζων αύτο απο του νομιχοϋ διχαίου. ού γάρ τω δόξαι τισίν η μη το φυσιχον διχαιον, αλλά το νομιχον ητοι πολιτιχόν το γάρ πολιτικον δίχαιον εξ αρχης μεν ούδεν διαφέρει, τεθεν δε και νομισθεν πολυ το διάφορον. το γάρ τον αδελφον μίγνυσθαι τη αδελφη εξ αρχης μεν αδιάφορον ην, νόμου δε τεθέντος μη μίγνυσθαι πολυ το διαφερον. χαι τους αιχμαλωτους πωλειν, ως βουλονται οι χεχρατηχοτες χαι διά ποίων, αδιάφορον ην. νόμου δε τεθέντος μια μνα πιπράσχειν, ούκ αλλως απεδίδουν ει μη δια μνας. το δε αίγα θύειν άλλά μη δύο πρόβατα ούχ απο ίστορίας ειληπται. χαι το θύειν η μη θύειν Βρασίδα αδιάφορον ετύγχανε. νόμου δε τεθέντος ώς ηρωϊ θύειν τον μη θύοντα εζημίουν. ού μόνον, φησί, ταυτα νομιχα δίχαιά εστιν, αλλά χαί οσα δια ψηφισμάτων προστάττουσι γίνεσθαι, χαί ταϋτα ούχ εστι των φύσει διχαίων, αλλά των νόμω και θέσει ήμετέρα γινομένων.

II.
Δοκεί δε ενίοις πάντα είναι τοιαυτα.

Διελων εις β το δίχαιον, εις το φυσιχον χαί το νομιχόν, λέγει οτι δοχεί τισι πάντα τά δίχαια νομιχά είναι, μηδεν δε φυσικόν, διότι παν φύσει αχίνητόν έστι (το γάρ πϋρ φύσει θερμον ον ούχ ενθάδε μέν εστι θερμόν, έν Αιγύπτω δε ου θερμόν, άλλά χαχεί χαι πανταχου), παν δε δίχαιον μεταπίπτει, ωστε ουδεν δίχαιον φύσει, αλλά παν δίχαιον νομιχον χαί πολιτιχον. ουτω θείς της δόξης την αιτίαν επάγει λέγων τουτο δ' ουχ εστιν ουτως εχον, άλλ' εστιν ώς ητοι ουχ εστιν αληθες άπλως οτι παν διχαιον κινείται, ώς λέγουσι τινες αλλ' εστιν ώς αχίνητόν έστι το δίχαιον. παρά γάρ τοίς Χατά φύσιν χαί αδιστρόφοις αχινητόν έστιν, ει χαί παρά τοίς χαχιστα διαχειμένοις χινείται. η ουν τουτό έστιν ο λέγει, η οτι ουχ εστιν άπλως αληθες οτι παν το φύσει αχίνητόν εστι. το γάρ φύσει πως μεν αχίνητόν έστιν, άπλως δε αχίνητον ουχ εστι. τη, μεν γάρ αυτου φύσει αχίνητον το φύσει, παρά δε τοίς μη χρωμένοις ώς πέφυκε χινούμενον. αμα δε διά τούτων γνωριμον γεγονε χαι πως ειπεν οτι φυσιχον εστι το πανταχου την αυτην εχον δύναμιν, οτι το πανταχου άντί του τοίς κατά φύσιν εχουσιν· έν απασι γαρ τοις χατα φυσιν εχουσι χαι μη διεστραμμενοις αχινητον το χατα φυσιν δίχαιον. χαί γάρ το φύσει άγαθόν αγαθόν έστιν, ώς παντας ώφελείν τους χατά φύσιν έχοντας, καί ουχ άπλως πάντας, ώς χαί το τη, έαυτοϋ φύσει γλυκυ γλυκύ εστιν, ώς γλυχάζειν απαντα; τους ύγιανοντας. το δε χαίτοι παρά γε τοίς θεοίς ουδαμως ίσως εχον προς την του Πλάτωνος δόξαν άπιδων είπε λέγοντος είναι χαι εν τοίς θεοίς δίχαιον, και προ αυτοϋ την αυτοδιχαιοσύνην. εί γαρ εστι, φησί, παρα τοίς θεοίς δίκαιον, τουτο ουδεποτε μεταπίπτει ουδέ αλλοις μεν των θεων έστιν αυτοδίχαιον αλλοις δ' ου τοιουτον, διά το πάντας αυτους όμοίως εχεινν. ουτως ουν εχει χαί επι των ανθρώπων. ει πάντες χατά φύσιν διέχειντο, ουχ αν μετέπιπτε το φύσει δίχαιον. ως γάρ εν τοίς χατα φύσιν εχουσιν η δεξια χείρ χρείττων χαί ίσχυροτέρα, έν δε τοίς παρα φύσιν ουχ ουτως, αλλ' ή αριστερά, διο χαι σπάνιοι οί τοιουτοι χαί ώς διποδές εσιν οί χατα φύσιν εχοντες χαι ώς δύο ωφθαλ'μους εχοντες, οί δε παρά φύσιν χαί τερατώδεις, ουχ ουτως, ουτω χαί έν τοίς χατά φύσιν εχουσιν ανθρώποις δίχαιόν έστι το φύσει δίχαιον. ωστε ου δεί την χρίσιν άπο των χαχως χαί παρά φύσιν διαχειμένων ποιείσθαι του φύσει διχαίου, αλλ' απο των χατά φύσιν εχόντων.εστι δη ουν παρ' ήμίν [χινητον] φύσει δίχαιον, χινητον μέντοι παν διά την των χρωμένων φαυλότητα χαί το παρά φύσιν διαχείσθαιι.

Ποίον δε φύσει των ένδεχομένων χαι αλλως έχειν χαι ποίον ου, αλλά νομιχον χαί συνθήχηκ.

Επεί, φησί, καί το φύσει δίχαιον μεταπίπτει χαί το νομιχόν (ει γαρ το φύσει, πολλω μαλλον το νομιχόν), τίνι γνωριοϋμεν οτι τόδε μεν ει χαι τάχα χεχίνηται, φυσιχόν έστι, τόδε δε νομιχόν; η ει χαί μήπω μεταπεπτώχασιν, ένδεχεται δε μεταπεσείν, πως διακρινουμεν το φυσιχον απο του νομιχου; χαί το μεν λεγόμενον τοιουτον, αυτος δε ουχ ουτως την λεξιν έπήνεγχε, χαί δια τουτο ασαφέστερόν πώς εστιν, αλλ' οίον αποφαινόμενος δηλον, φησίν, έστί ποίον δίχαιόν έστι φύσει, χαι ποίον νομιχόν, χαίτοι ένδεχομένων αμφοτέρων άλλως εχειν. Διορισ-θήσεται γαρ, φησίν, απο των αλλων. ώς γαρ έπ' έχείνων απο των χατά φύσιν έχόντων χρίνεται, ποία χείρ έστι χρείττων, οτι ή δεξιά, χαί ποία χείρων, οτι ή αριστερά, χαίτοι ενδέχεται χαι ταίς χερσίν αμφοτέραις ισον τινα ισχύειν, ουτω χαι το φύσει δίχαιον, ει Χαί μεταπίπτειν ένδεχεται, απο των χατα φύσιν έχόντων χρινουμεν οτι τοιουτόν έστιν, ει χαί μη τοίς παρά φύσιν διαχειμένοις ισχύει. ταυτα ειπων διά των επαγομένων ενδείχνυται, πως το χατα συνθήχαν δίχαιον τίθεται Χαί παλιν μετατιθεται. ώς γαρ τά μετρα φησί προς το χρήσιμον αλλάττεται, ουτω χαι το χατά συνθήχην δίχαιον την αρχην μεν τιθεται δια το δοχείν συμφέρειν τω Χοινω, επειτα μεταπίπτει, ηνίχα δοχεί μη συμφέρειν η οπου μη συμφέρει. ου γαρ το συμφέρον τη δημοχρατία συμφέρει Χαι τη ολιγαρχία η τη αριστοχρατία. ωστε επεί αλλο μεν το δίχαιον χαι το συμφέρον τη δημοκρατία, άλλο δε τη αριστοχρατία, έπειδαν ή πολιτεία οίον ή δημοχρατία μεταπέση εις αριστοχρατίαν η αυτη εις εχείνην δι' ας αιτίας λέγει έν ταις Πολιτείαις τας μεταπτώσεις αυτων γίνεσθαι, ανάγχη χαί τά νομιχά δίχαια μεταπίπτειν. οϋχ εισι δε πανταχου χαί παρα πασιν αί αυταί πολιτεία, διότι μη φύσει αλλά νομω χαί χατά συνθήχην συνίστανται χαί χρωνται χαί διχαίοις τοιούτοις· ή μέντοι αρίστη πολιτεία (ητις δέ έστιν αυτη, είρηχεν έν ταίς πολιτείαις) αεί χαί παρά πασιν τοίς χατα φύσιν εχουσιν ή αυτή έστι.

Georgios Pachymeres[13]

I.
<u>Τοῦ δὲ πολιτικοῦ δικαίου τὸ μὲν φυσικόν ἐστι τὸ δὲ νομικὸν· φυσικὸν μὲν τὸ πανταχοῦ τὴν αὐτὴν ἔχον δύναμιν·</u> δοκεῖ γὰρ πᾶσιν ἐσθίειν πεινάσαντας καὶ μὴ ἑαυτοὺς αὐθεντεῖν καὶ φονεύειν, τὸ τὸν πατέρα τιμᾶν, τὸ ἐπαρκεῖν τοῖς ἐνδεέσι, τὸ τὸν θεὸν σέβειν, καὶ τὰ τοιαῦτα· τὸ δὲ νομικὸν μὴ τεθὲν <u>μὲν οὐδὲν διαφέρει</u>, κἂν οὕτω πράξοι τις κἂν ἄλλως· τεθὲν δὲ βέβαιόν ἐστιν, ὡς τὸ <u>λυτροῦσθαι</u> μὴ ἐπέκεινα μνᾶς τὸν ἑαλωκότα, καὶ τὸ <u>αἶγα θύειν ἀλλὰ μὴ πρόβατα</u>, καὶ ἄλλα μυρία ἐπὶ τοῖς καθέκαστα.

---

[13] Xenophontos 2022, pp. 210-213.

II.

ἄλλοι δὲ ἄλλως διαιροῦσιν, ὅτι τὸ μὲν φυσικὸν ἀκίνητον, κινεῖται δὲ τὸ νόμιμον. τοῦτο δὲ οὐκ ἔστιν οὕτως, ἀλλ᾽ ἔστι καὶ φυσικὸν κινητόν· οὐ πᾶν δέ.

III.

Ἔπειτα δὲ ἐρωτᾷ ὅτι, εἴπερ καὶ ἄμφω κινητά, ποῖόν ἐστιν ἐν τοῖς φυσικοῖς τὸ ἐνδεχόμενον κινεῖσθαι, καὶ ποῖον οὔ. εὕρηται γοῦν φύσει κρείττων ἡ δεξιά, ἀλλὰ πολλοῖς παρακεκίνηται τοῦτο, καί εἰσιν ἢ ἀμφιδέξιοι ἢ ἀριστερόχειρες· καὶ εἴ τινές εἰσιν, ἐνδέχεται καὶ πάντας τοιούτους γίνεσθαι. τὰ δὲ κατὰ συνθήκην τῶν δικαίων, ἐπεὶ πρὸς τὸ συνοῖσον μετατίθενται, ὅμοιά εἰσι τοῖς μέτροις, ᾧ πωλοῦσι καὶ ᾧ ἐξωνοῦνταί τινες, ὡς τοὺς αὐτοὺς μείζω μὲν ἔχειν ἐν τῷ ὠνεῖσθαι, ἐλάττω δὲ ἐν τῷ πωλεῖν.

Ὁμοίως καὶ πολλὰ τοιαῦτά εἰσι ⟨μὴ⟩ φυσικὰ ἀλλὰ ἀνθρώπινα καὶ οὐ διήκοντα καὶ εἰς ἄλλα ζῷα· οἱ γὰρ ἄνθρωποι μόνοι πολιτεύονται, καὶ αἱ πολιτεῖαι τούτων διάφοροι, ὧν μία ὡσανεὶ κατὰ φύσιν ἡ ἀρίστη.[14] τῶν δὲ δικαίων καὶ νομίμων ἕκαστον ὡς τὸ καθόλου πρὸς τὰ καθέκαστα ἔχει· τὰ μὲν γὰρ πραττόμενα πολλὰ καὶ καθέκαστα, τὸ δὲ ἕν· καθόλου γάρ· δημοκρατία ἴσως ἢ ἀριστοκρατία ἢ βασιλεία· τούτων γὰρ ἕκαστον ἕν· καὶ τὸ μὲν δίκαιον ἑκάστης πολιτείας ἕν, πολλὰ δὲ κατ᾽ αὐτὸ τὰ συμπίπτοντα.

---

[14] Here marks the conclusion of the passage I have cited in the other commentaries and translations. Nonetheless, given the significance of this passage in comprehending the connection between the commentaries of Georgios and Michael, I have chosen to include the subsequent two phrases.

CHAPTER SEVEN: LATIN COMMENTARIES

There exist over fifteen Latin medieval commentaries on the *Nicomachean Ethics*, some of which include a commentary on book V.[1] In this chapter, we will provide summaries for three significant scholastic commentaries (those by Albertus Magnus, Thomas Aquinas, and Geraldus Odonis),[2] and introduce an example from the

---

[1] For a comprehensive list of these commentaries, please refer to Wieland 1982. Additionally, for insights into the reception of Aristotle's *Nicomachean Ethics* at the Faculty of Arts in Paris before and after 1277, consult Costa 2012. For a broader overview of the question of natural law and natural right, Luscombe 1982. Additionally, Fuchs 2017, pp. 62-214.

[2] It is also essential to mention Jean Buridan's *Quaestiones super decem libros Ethicorum Aristotelis ad Nicomachum*, specifically questions XIX-XX (J. Buridan, "Questions sur l'Ethique à Nicomaque, livre V", transcribed by F. Pironet, pp. 155-168). I would like to express my gratitude to Robert Andrew for providing me with this transcription. Regarding Buridan's perspective on natural law, there is a comprehensive exploration in García-Huidobro 2015. These two questions by Buridan delve into general inquiries concerning the definitions of divine laws, natural law, conventional (or legal) law, political justice, legal justice, and natural justice. They also explore the divergence between *jus*, *justum*, and *legem*. Buridan offers several definitions for each term and addresses various questions by applying his definitions. Buridan's analysis, though extensive and intricate, does not share a profound connection with Aristotle's text under examination and is thoroughly discussed in the aforementioned article. For these reasons, I have chosen not to delve into his views within the scope of this book. However, it is noteworthy

Latin Averroist commentaries through the work of Raoul le Breton.³

Albertus Magnus

Albertus Magnus (1206-1280) authored two distinct works pertaining to the *Ethics*, namely, a paraphrase closely aligned with the Latin text of Robert Grosseteste and a commentary that has been included in both versions of the *Opera omnia*, encompassing various treatises.⁴ Notably, the latter commentary serves as a

---

that Buridan incorporates, in some of his definitions, Thomas Aquinas's view that natural law provides the principles for conventional law. Buridan also aligns with Thomas's viewpoint that conventional laws can vary in quality, depending on how effectively they facilitate human attainment of their natural perfection.

[3] Regarding this Averroist trend of commentators, see Gauthier 1948 and Costa 2012.

[4] I have used Borgnet's edition of the *Opera omnia*, (Paris, 1890-1899) as the primary source, specifically, the commentaries relevant to the *Ethics* which can be found in volume VII (Paris, 1891), pp. 366-71. For an in-depth exploration of Albertus Magnus's perspective on natural law through his diverse writings, including *De bono* and his commentary on the *Ethics*, we recommend reference to Cunningham 1967, as well as Fuchs 2017, pp. 80-137. Both Cunningham and Fuchs delve into the intricate relationship between conventional (legal) and natural law in the writings of Albertus Magnus. They converge in the understanding that conventional (legal) law represents a specific manifestation of natural law, subject to variations across time and place in its specific form, while the fundamental categories remain constant and aligned with the natural law paradigm. It is essential to acknowledge, however, that my interpretation of Albertus Magnus's treatise is distinct from theirs. A comprehensive exploration of Albert's stance on this matter would exceed

compendium of passages addressing diverse ethical subjects, with particular relevance to our subject matter. Two of these passages assume paramount significance for our analysis: the third chapter of the third treatise on the *Ethics* (De justo politico et naturali) and the fourth chapter of the same treatise (De errore qui justum naturale non unius omnes determinant). In this examination, we shall focus exclusively on this commentary, as it exhibits a closer connection to our chosen topic and exerts a profound influence on subsequent Latin commentaries.

Albert's commentary on our chosen text exhibits a distinctive structure, comprising two distinct sections. The first section is dedicated to the examination of the first passage, while the second section addresses the second and third passages. Albert's commentary, rather than conforming to the conventional format of a comprehensive commentary on Aristotle's text, adopts a different approach. It assumes the form of a catalogue of

---

the scope of this book. Notably, though, the two scholars who have conducted a thorough investigation into Albertus Magnus's views have not identified substantial discrepancies among his various works addressing our subject.

It is, further, worth noting that while the first commentary has not yet undergone rigorous scholarly editing and is presently unavailable to me, it remains an area of potential future research. Additionally, it is conceivable that Thomas Aquinas's viewpoints may well have influenced the interpretation of Albertus Magnus by certain scholars. This avenue of inquiry holds promise for future investigation.

philosophical inquiries that directly pertain to Aristotle's text. This particular approach results in Albert's omission of certain portions of Aristotle's original text, as not every part is explicitly referenced in his commentary. Consequently, in our analysis, we shall proceed by initially providing a summary of Albert's perspective as conveyed in this commentary. Subsequently, we will elucidate the way he interprets select passages from Aristotle, sometimes even without direct quotation, thereby highlighting his distinctive approach to the text.

At the outset of the first question (chapter III) and at the conclusion of the second question (chapter IV), Albert delineates a tripartite classification for the various types of laws. These categories can be summarized as follows:

1. Laws that are exclusively conventional in nature.
2. Laws that are purely natural.
3. Laws that constitute customs, representing a fusion of both natural and conventional elements.

This distinction between the two kinds of categories becomes particularly evident in the opening section of chapter III.

Politici autem justi in contrarium quidem duae sunt species, quamvis plures sint modi. Una quidem species naturale justum: alia autem justum legale. Naturale autem dicimus, quod simpliciter naturale est, nullam legalis justi habens admixtionem. Legale autem, quod	However, concerning the just actions of politicians, there are indeed two species, although there are many variations. One species is the natural just, while the other is the legal just. We call it natural when it is purely natural, without any mixture of the legal just. And we call

simpliciter legale est, nihil habet admixtum.	it legal when it is purely legal, without any mixture.

Following this conceptual delineation, Albert proceeds to expound upon Aristotle's definitions pertaining to each category of law. According to Aristotle, natural law remains uniform and consistent across all contexts, while conventional laws are contingent upon the determinations made by legislators for the collective welfare of the populace "ex ratione utilitatis communis".[5] Prior to their formal establishment through legislation, these laws do not bear inherent endorsement, nor are their violations subject to punishment. However, once legislatively enacted, individuals are obliged to adhere to these laws, and transgressions thereof incur punitive measures.

The elucidation of the third category of justice or laws, namely, customs, can be found in the subsequent sections of the third chapter.

Ex his patet quod consuetudinis medium est inter legale et naturale, scilicet quod a natura profectum.	From these things, it is evident that custom is a middle ground between the legal and the natural, namely that which has arisen from nature.

Customs, as delineated by Albert, are laws that possess a natural foundation and have been formally acknowledged

---

[5] Albert notes that legislators can be categorized into three distinct types: the wise, the general populace, or the princes. These various categories of legislators correspond to the three diverse forms of government: aristocracy, democracy, and monarchy.

as laws by legislative authorities. Alternatively, customs may be interpreted as laws stemming from overarching natural principles, with their specific applications being determined by legislators.

Moreover, in his commentary, Albert also introduces a distinction between six distinct categories of natural law. It is noteworthy that Thomasand Geraldus (as Buridan), in their subsequent works, continue to develop and refine this distinction, albeit in a manner distinct from Albert's approach. This categorization, encompassing various types of natural laws and, subsequently, different types of conventional laws, emerges as a distinctive feature within the tradition of Latin commentaries. Importantly, it sets the Latin commentary tradition apart from the Greek, Arabic, and Hebrew traditions of commenting on Aristotle's *Ethics*.[6]

Within his exposition of natural laws, Albert references the viewpoints articulated by Michael (and the Aristotelian commentator Eustratius)[7] and proceeds to elucidate his dissenting view.

---

[6] The examination of the various categories of natural law diverges from a direct engagement with Albert's interpretation of Aristotle's text and, instead, delves into the realm of Albert's ethical viewpoints. Consequently, we will abstain from individually scrutinizing the diverse classifications of natural law offered by each Latin commentator. Elucidating these discrepancies would necessitate a comprehensive analysis of the ethical writings of these commentators, an endeavor that exceeds the scope of this book.

[7] The commentary by Eustratius of Nicaea on the fifth chapter of the *Nicomachean Ethics* has regrettably been lost to history. However, insights gleaned from Albert suggest that Eustratius' perspective likely bore a striking resemblance to that of Michael.

Sic ergo intelligitur quod justum naturale ubique eamdem habet potentiam et quod non consistit in videri vel non videri. Potentiam autem dicimus, primam inclinationem ex natura rationali, et non illam quae accipitur in effectu. Quamvis enim apud Trivallos pium sit interficere parentes, tamen hoc non dictat natura de parente secundum quod parens est: sed ad hoc mala consuetudo provexit ex ratione male arguens, scilicet quod magis pium sit parentem miserum miseriam cito finire, quam in miseria diu vivere. Unde etiam apud abutentes jure naturali prima principia ejusdem potentiae sunt, cujus sunt apud bene utentes. Et ideo imperfectum est dictum Eustratii et Michaelis Ephesii, qui dicunt justum naturale non esse ejusdem potentire, nisi apud bene utentes ipso secundum naturam. Apud bestialiter autem viventes, nullam dicunt esse potentiam justi naturalis. Homo enim quamdiu homo est, principiis humanis non destituitur.

Thus, it is understood that natural justice has the same power everywhere and that it does not depend on appearances. By power, we mean the primary inclination derived from rational nature, not the one that is observed in its effects. Although, according to the Trivalles, it may be considered pious to kill one's parents, nature does not dictate this regarding a parent insofar as they are a parent. It is through a corrupt custom, based on faulty reasoning, that such a notion has arisen, arguing that it is more pious to quickly end the misery of a miserable parent than that he [the parent] live in misery for a long time. Therefore, even among those who abuse natural law, the fundamental principles of the same power exist as they do among those who use it properly. Thus, the statements of Eustratius and Michael of Ephesus, claiming that natural justice does not possess the same power except among those who use it well according to nature, are imperfect. Among the savages, they say that there is no power of natural justice. For as long as a

> person remains human, they are not deprived of their human principles.

Within this text, we acquire insight into Albert's perspective, which posits that there exist individuals who do not adhere to the principles of natural justice and law. Nevertheless, Albert explicitly rejects Michael's notion that certain populations, deemed naturally inferior, are incapable of abiding by natural law. In Albert's view, natural law is universally accessible to all human beings, and any failure to observe these laws is considered a moral transgression. He emphasizes that even in circumstances marked by great suffering for one's parents, it remains impermissible to commit acts such as patricide. Natural laws, according to Albert, are inherently just and applicable across all scenarios in all human societies.

Albert firmly asserts that human nature retains an enduring capacity to adhere to natural law, a capacity that cannot be forfeited. He contends that even those considered "savage" possess the potential to transform their societies into ones characterized by a more conventional adherence to natural justice and laws.

Chapter III offers valuable insights into Albert's conception of natural law, which encompasses a wide array of significant topics, including, echoing Cicero's words, "religio, pietas, gratia, vindicatio, observantia, et veritas" (religion, piety, gratitude, retribution, observance, and truth). It is essential to underscore, however, that Albert distinguishes between laws derived from divine revelation and those classified as natural law. Natural law emanates from human reason, while divine laws, according to Albert, exist, "cum quaedam eorum et supra rationem sunt, quaedam autem praeter rationem valde, quaedam etiam contra rationem inveniuntur" (beyond reason, some greatly surpass reason, and some even contradict reason).

In Albert's view, natural law encompasses the concept of religion, signifying the recognition of the need for some form of religiosity. However, it does not encompass specific divine laws, as these extend beyond the bounds of reason and, consequently, the realm of natural law.

Remarkably, Albert introduces a novel element to the foundational Aristotelian distinctions between natural and conventional law—a third category known as divine law. This innovation significantly shapes the trajectory of subsequent Latin commentators and exerts influence on later Jewish commentators. This augmentation derives from the monotheistic context shared by Albert and other medieval scholars. However, it is important to note that not all monotheistic thinkers deem it necessary to incorporate divine law as a third category in their interpretations of Aristotelian ethics. This concept does not appear in the interpretations of Arabic and Greek commentators, as well as in those Jewish commentators who remain unaffected by the Latin tradition of commentaries. For instance, Averroes notes that laws related to the divine, such as the regulation of prayers and religious services (ut commensuratio orationum et servitiorum in qualibet lege / כמו שעירת התפלות והעבודות בדת), fall within the realm of conventional laws, thereby differing from Albert's approach.

In the fourth chapter, Albert references a perspective held by certain individuals who contend that there is no such thing as natural law, positing that everything is natural, akin to the universally inherent quality of fire to burn in all environments. Albert acknowledges this viewpoint, conceding that there is no law comparable to the unvarying nature of fire. He further asserts that natural law can undergo alterations to a certain extent. Nevertheless, he stipulates that these changes are confined to human affairs, emphasizing that divine laws remain unchanging and immutable.

Unde quamvis apud deos omne justum nequaquam aliter se habeat, eo quod nihil diis mutabile est: apud nos autem natura ens aliquo modo mutabile est, quia omne quod in natura humana est, mutabile est: et quamvis hoc sit, tamen humanorum justorum aliquod est naturale, aliquod non naturale.	Therefore, although all just things do not vary among the gods, since nothing is subject to change for the gods, in our case, nature is to some extent changeable because everything within human nature is subject to change. And although this is the case, there are certain just things among humans that are natural and others that are not natural.

Within this text, it becomes evident that natural law retains its intrinsic character independently of the alterations influenced by human practice. As the text progresses, Albert further notes the existence of a select few peoples, specifically the Zabadreai and the Bragmanni, who possess laws that correspond perfectly with the principles of natural law.

These examples shed light on the existence of natural law among human societies, a law that is intended to be applied universally across all communities. Nevertheless, each society undergoes a process of adaptation, tailoring specific laws derived from the universal natural law to suit the demands of their unique temporal, geographical, and cultural contexts. It is important to acknowledge that even among these various applications of natural laws within diverse societies, inherent natural differences persist. Certain specific legal implications remain closely aligned with the principles of natural justice and laws, while others exhibit more pronounced deviations. Moreover, there are exceptional instances where individuals or communities may possess specific laws that are entirely congruent with the principles of natural law.

Towards the conclusion of the fourth chapter, Albert proceeds to expound upon the disparities that exist between the universal components of laws and those that are specific in nature:

Justorum autem legalium omnium sive naturalia sint, sive legalia sive consuetudenalia unumquodque sic se habet ut universale ad particularia. Universale enim in multis et de multis est secundum rationem non variatum, et sic est de multis: et cum multa sint in quibus est magnam et multimodam secundum esse habet variationem. Per omnem eumdem modum est in his quae justa sunt, quae sunt mensura operum nostrorum. Operata enim ab hominibus valde multa et differentia sunt; Justorum autem sive naturalium sive legalium	However, concerning the laws of the just, whether they pertain to the natural realm, the legal realm, or the realm of customs, each one is such that the universal relates to the particular. For the universal, in its many aspects and from many perspectives, remains unchanged in accordance with reason, and thus it applies to many things. However, since there are many things in which it exists with great variation and diversity according to its essence, it applies in the same manner to those things which are just and serve as the measure of our actions.

quod mensura operatum est, unumquodque est unum secundum se et rationem. Sic enim mensurando universale est, et de multis secundum quod ponitur in usu, non omnia sibi aequaliter applicabilia invenit : et ideo in usu necesse est variari, qui a sic non de multis, sed in multis est.	Indeed, the works of humans are highly numerous and diverse. Yet, regarding the laws of the just, whether they pertain to the natural realm or the legal realm, the measure of action is one for each, according to its own nature and reason. For it is in this manner that the universal is measured and, as it is applied in practice, it does not find all things equally applicable to it. Therefore, in practice, it is necessary for it to vary, as it is not only for a select few but for many.

In this passage, Albert asserts that within the realms of all three types of laws — natural, conventional, and customary — there exists a duality: a universal component that remains constant and a specific component that undergoes adaptation in accordance with the requirements of those who practice these laws. It is my contention that this passage does not contradict the earlier assertion that natural law remains consistent across all places and times, while conventional laws are subject to change. Albert addresses distinct facets of immutability and variability in both passages. In our interpretation, conventional laws exhibit the capacity for alteration between different societies, marked by variations in temporal and geographical contexts, thus rendering them distinct yet equivalent.

However, within each society, the specific application of these laws must adapt to suit the needs of the individuals practicing the law in every specific circumstance. To illustrate, in a society that has chosen to offer a female goat as an offering to Brasidas,[8] there may arise exceptional circumstances where it becomes necessary to sacrifice a cow due to an unusual increase in the cost of goats during that specific period and location — a rarity rather than the norm.

In contrast, natural law remains constant in its universal principles across all places and times, as well as in its preferred specific applications. Nevertheless, many human societies fail to adhere to the optimal implementation of natural law in all their specific legal enactments, often altering the specific applications of the law to align with their unique circumstances, temporal considerations, and cultural factors. It is worth noting that certain societies, regrettably, may not practice aspects of the universal principles of natural law. These modifications do not arise from any inherent inferiority that renders these individuals' incapable of grasping natural law but rather stem from misguided decisions or insufficient examination on the part of the people and legislators within that specific society. In the majority of cases, these alterations affect only the specific implications of natural laws but leave the universal principles intact. The separation between the universal and specific within natural law represents a divergence from the natural good. In contrast, changes in specific conventional laws signify deviations from established legislated norms.

---

[8] Brasidas was a Spartan general who was honoured as one of the founders of the city of Amphipolis, which he had helped to free from Athenian power.

In summary, Albert posits that natural law is constituted by inherent natural principles, both in its overarching principles and specific applications. Conversely, conventional law is inherently contingent, encompassing both its fundamental principles and specific applications. However, a noteworthy distinction emerges within each category, with a clear demarcation between universal principles that remain constant (for conventional law, across various societies, and for natural law, in the practice of the majority of societies) and specific applications that tend to vary over time and across different contexts.

Notably, Albert does not introduce the distinction, which subsequently appears in Thomas's commentary and is perpetuated in subsequent Latin commentaries, between natural law, which establishes general principles, and conventional laws, which pertain solely to the specific application of these general principles.

Regarding the debate between relativism and natural law, Albert aligns with the perspective that posits the existence of an objectively superior natural law. This interpretation aligns with the trend initiated by the initial Latin translation of Aristotle and establishes a trajectory that would also influence his student, Thomas Aquinas.

Thomas Aquinas

Undoubtedly, Thomas Aquinas (1225-1274) stands out as the preeminent medieval Catholic philosopher. His view on natural law holds paramount significance, profoundly influencing all subsequent explorations of this subject. In this chapter, our focus is exclusively on his commentary pertaining to the same text by Aristotle, without attempting to provide a comprehensive summary of his broader stance on natural law—a topic that has been extensively examined in numerous books and articles.⁹ Furthermore, we shall elucidate the profound impact he has exerted on subsequent Latin and Hebrew commentaries on this text.

Aquinas main contribution lies in the definition of conventional or legal laws as a specific subset of universal natural principles. This concept is absent in the original Aristotelian text and is likely inspired by the works of both Averroes and Cicero. It subsequently gains widespread acceptance in later medieval Latin commentaries and leaves its mark on Jewish commentators.

Furthermore, Thomas advances the notion that within the realm of conventional laws, there exist variations in terms of their alignment with natural principles — an idea not explicitly articulated in the Aristotelian text. This interpretation draws on Aristotle's examples but is not explicitly expressed in Aristotle's work. It is probable that this perspective is influenced, at least in part, by the commentary of Albertus Magnus. Interestingly, in Albertus Magnus's commentary, the differentiation between universal principles of justice and law and their specific applications does not neatly align with the distinction between natural and conventional law.¹⁰

---

9   For an in-depth examination of Thomas Aquinas's perspective on natural law, one may consult to the following scholarly sources: Fuchs 2017, pp. 138-214; Sweeney 2012; Lisska 1997. Thomas's primary exposition of his views on natural law are found in his *Summa theologiae* Ia IIae, q. 91-97.

10 As an illustration, consider the subject of equity. It is not within the scope of this discussion to conduct an exhaustive analysis of the impact of Aquinas on the development of Christian and Jewish philosophical perspectives concerning equity. However, I

I.

At the outset of his commentary on the first passage, Thomas Aquinas expounds upon the evolution of the Aristotelian text and elucidates the diverse connotations of the term "just." The Doctor Angelicus further discerns two distinct meanings of natural justice (or laws):

1. *In terms of effects:* natural law remains consistent universally, irrespective of geographical or temporal variations.

2. *In terms of origin:* natural law emanates from human nature.

Thomas proceeds to make two distinctions within the concept of human nature: according to one, human nature as akin to other animals; according to the other human nature is portrayed as rational animals necessitating societal structures. The ambit of natural laws encompasses both conceptions.

Furthermore, Thomas introduces a third categorization within legal justice (or law):

1. *Matters that are neutral prior to legislation:* these are actions or behaviours that are neither prohibited nor recommended until formally legislated upon. This form of legislation, notably the only one explicitly mentioned by Aristotle, encompasses actions that transition from neutrality to either prohibition or recommendation only after legislation.

anticipate conducting in-depth research in this area during the near future, to explore the influence of Thomas Aquinas particularly within the realm of Jewish philosophy-

2. *Specific legislation pertaining to individual cases:* this involves legislation crafted for specific individuals or scenarios.

3. *Legal justice formulated by judges that acquires the force of legislation:* in this case, the judgments made by judges assume the authority of legislation.

While these distinctions hold significant importance, it is essential to note that they do not have a direct correlation with the text of Aristotle, which constitutes the primary focus of this book. Thomas primarily appends these distinctions, which are extant in the writings of other philosophers and legal scholars, to the first category present in Aristotle's text.

These distinctions are related but not identical to the division articulated by Albert, and this manner of interpretation forms a distinctive hallmark of Latin commentary. The subsequent sections of Thomas's commentary on the first passage bear substantial relevance to the overarching theme of natural law.

Est autem hic considerandum, quod iustum legale sive positivum oritur semper a naturali, ut Tullius dicit in sua rhetorica. Dupliciter tamen aliquid potest oriri a iure naturali. Uno modo sicut conclusio ex principiis; et sic ius positivum vel legale non potest oriri a iure naturali; praemissis enim existentibus, necesse est conclusionem esse; sed cum iustum naturale sit semper et ubique, ut dictum est, hoc non competit iusto

However, it must be considered that legal or positive justice always arises from natural justice, as Tully states in his *Rhetoric*. Nevertheless, something can arise from natural law in two ways. Firstly, as a conclusion derived from principles, and in this way, positive or legal law cannot arise from natural law. For when the premises exist, the conclusion is necessarily reached. But since natural justice is always and

legali vel positivo. Et ideo necesse est quod quicquid ex iusto naturali sequitur, quasi conclusio, sit iustum naturale; sicut ex hoc quod est nulli esse iniuste nocendum, sequitur non esse furandum, quod item ad ius naturale pertinet.

everywhere, as mentioned before, it does not belong to legal or positive justice. Therefore, whatever follows as a conclusion from natural justice is itself natural justice. For example, from the principle that it is unjust to harm others, it follows that stealing is unjust, which also pertains to natural law.

Alio modo oritur aliquid ex iusto naturali per modum determinationis; et sic omnia iusta positiva vel legalia ex iusto naturali oriuntur. Sicut furem esse puniendum est iustum naturale, sed quod sit etiam puniendum tali vel tali poena, hoc est lege positum.

Secondly, something can arise from natural justice through determination, and in this way, all positive or legal just actions originate from natural justice. For instance, it is natural justice that a thief should be punished, but the specific punishment assigned to the thief is established by positive law.

Attendendum est etiam quod iustum legale dupliciter oritur a naturali secundum modum praedictum. Uno modo cum permixtione. Alio modo sine permixtione alicuius humani erroris, et hoc etiam exempla Aristotilis demonstrant; naturaliter enim iustum est quod civi non ob suam culpam oppresso subveniatur et per consequens quod captivus redimatur: taxatio autem pretii, quae pertinet ad iustum legale, procedit ex praedicto

It should also be noted that legal justice can arise from natural justice in two ways, as mentioned above. Firstly, it can arise with a mixture of natural justice [and human error]. Secondly, it can arise without any admixture of human error, as demonstrated by Aristotle's examples. Naturally, it is just that aid be given to a citizen who is oppressed through no fault of their own, and consequently, it is just that a captive be re-

iusto naturali absque omni errore. Est etiam naturale iustum quod benefactori honor exhibeatur; sed quod honor divinus exhibeatur homini est ex errore humano et tale est quod sacrificetur Brasidae. Sententialia vero iusta sunt applicationes iustorum legalium ad particularia facta.	deemed. However, the determination of the price, which falls under legal justice, proceeds from the aforementioned natural justice without any error. It is also naturally just that honor be bestowed upon a benefactor, but the offering of divine honor to a human being is due to human error, such as the sacrifice to Brasidas. Sentences of the court, on the other hand, are just applications of legal just actions to specific cases.[11]

In this passage, we examine the relationship between conventional (legal) justice and law in relation to natural justice and law, as articulated by Thomas. It is asserted that conventional laws cannot be regarded as a direct derivation of natural law. Rather, the conclusion reached through conventional law is of the same nature as the principles from which it derives. Consequently, when a specific law is deduced from natural law, it is intrinsically connected to natural law.

---

[11] An English translation of this particular passage from Thomas's commentary on the *Ethics* can be found at https://aquinas.cc/la/en/~Eth.Bk5.L12. However, I have not preferred not to use this translation due to my disagreement with certain decisions made by the translator. For instance, the choice to render *iure naturali* as "natural right" instead of "natural law." Additionally, this translation introduces alterations to the concluding part of the quoted passage, omitting the name of Brasidas and simply mentioning the prohibition of worshipping a human as God.

Conventional law serves as the particular manifestation of those natural principles that are not inherently natural in themselves. For instance, while it is a natural inclination to punish a thief, the precise determination of the punishment is not inherently dictated by nature and may vary based on legislative decisions. Thomas further posits that legislators can err when formulating specific laws derived from natural principles. An illustrative example is the act of offering sacrifices to individuals perceived as benefactors of society, as in the case of Brasidas. Honouring benefactors is a component of natural law, but the specific form of homage, such as making sacrifices to them, represents an erroneous interpretation.

From this perspective, it becomes evident that there exist both appropriate and inappropriate approaches, guided by natural principles, to enact specific legislation. The practice of sacrificing to Brasidas, while stemming from genuine natural principles, runs counter to other aspects of natural law, possibly such as the principle of worshipping only one God. Consequently, it is deemed a misguided and unjust legislation, despite its derivation from authentic natural principles.

II.

In his commentary on the second passage, Thomas closely aligns his interpretation with Aristotle's text, arguing against philosophers who assert that there is no concept of natural justice due to the variability observed in human justice. According to Thomas, there is indeed change within the realm of natural justice, occurring either essentially or accidentally ("vel per se vel per accidens"). However, the fundamental categories of natural and conventional law persist as distinct entities. It is worth noting that matters pertaining to separated intellectual or celestial substances exhibit a notable stability and lack of change. Conversely, all elements related to human affairs are susceptible to fluctuations, yet despite this inherent variability, certain aspects of them maintain their inherent character as being aligned with the principles of natural law.

III.

In the analysis of the third passage, Thomas provides insights into how natural phenomena can undergo change while retaining their fundamental essence. Initially, he expounds upon the idea that certain natural phenomena hold true as a general rule, yet specific circumstances may render them inapplicable. To illustrate the point, Thomas makes reference to a renowned example from Plato's *Republic*, where the act of returning an item to a friend is regarded as virtuous, while returning a weapon to an intoxicated friend is not. Thomas interprets this example, involving the concept of the right hand, within the context of the example from the *Republic*. In accordance with his view, the presence of individuals who may be ambidextrous or exhibit a preference for their left hand does not fundamentally alter the inherent nature of the superiority of the right hand.

From his interpretation of this example, it becomes evident that Thomas regards exceptions to natural laws as arising from unfavourable circumstances. It is important to note that this perspective does not originate from Aristotle's text but rather from the illustrative example drawn from Plato's work. This perspective is further reinforced by Thomas's explicit description of exceptions, as he states, "sed ut in paucioribus deficiunt". At this juncture, Thomas bears a resemblance to the anonymous Greek commentators (as well as Michael of Ephesus).

Thomas introduces a pivotal distinction between two distinct categories of natural laws. The first category comprises natural laws derived from the rational part of human nature, which remain unalterable in all circumstances. Conversely, the second category encompasses natural laws emanating from the more primal, animalistic aspects of human existence, subject to modification under specific conditions. This differentiation, conspicuously absent within Aristotelian literature, assumes profound importance for the prospective development of Latin commentaries.[12]

Thomas likely intends to convey that laws aimed at perfecting human intellect, offering legal advantages to the intellectually inclined, exhibit uniformity across geographical and cultural boundaries. In contrast, natural laws contingent upon the animalistic dimensions of human nature, such as those governing the permissibility of multiple spouses, may exhibit regional variability. While the union of male and female is inherently natural, the specific norms regulating such unions may undergo

---

[12] For instance, Geraldus and Buridan both embraced this distinction and further elaborated upon it by introducing additional distinctions. According to Poblete 2018 and 2020, this development was initially influenced by Grosseteste's translation, subsequently impacting Albertus, and ultimately Thomas. Whilst this assertion holds true, it is important to note that Thomas's approach differs and is more radical than the interpretation provided by earlier Latin commentators. Furthermore, Thomas's perspective exerts a profound influence on subsequent commentators.

alteration. According to Thomas, one of these approaches, monogamy, may be deemed superior.

Thomas proceeds to expound that there exist fundamental natural principles that remain immutable in all circumstances, alongside others that may undergo variations contingent upon the unique constitutional framework of each nation. He concludes the commentary by positing the existence of an ideal constitution — one in complete alignment with natural principles. This constitution, he suggests, adheres perfectly to natural law and provides its inhabitants with an optimal state of affairs, necessitating no deviations from it. Upon closer examination of the commentary on the first passage, it becomes apparent that even within such an ideal constitutional framework, certain conventional regulations can exist that hold no inherent bias. These particular regulations likely pertain to highly specific scenarios, such as the precise penalties for theft.

Conclusion

In summary, Thomas contributes a significant interpretation that would come to shape future approaches to commentary on this particular chapter of Aristotle. He posits that conventional legal laws represent specific manifestations of underlying natural law principles—a position influenced by both Cicero and Averroes, but one that Thomas articulates with greater coherence. Among these legal laws, some are entirely neutral, permitting the existence of distinct yet equivalent legal norms. Nevertheless, Thomas acknowledges the possibility of human fallibility in the application of natural law, resulting in deviations from the intended outcomes. Such deviations, he contends, run counter to the dictates of natural law, thereby rendering the specific legal implications incorrect. In such instances, a contradiction emerges between the conventional law, which is erroneous according to the principles of natural law.[13] Consequently, Thomas contends that there exists a superlative conventional law—one that remains free from errors in its alignment with natural law principles.

Radulphus Brito

Radulphus Brito (1270-1320 was a grammarian who lectured and held the position of master of arts at the University of Paris.[14] His commentary, which we will examine in this study, aligns with the broader trend of commentaries associated with the Averroist school of thought on ethics. It is essential to acknowledge that characterizing these commentaries as unequivocally Averroist is a matter of academic contention, the exploration of which falls beyond the scope of this book.[15]

Radulphus's commentary on our text comprises questions 126 to 128 of his larger commentary on Aristotle's *Ethics*. Among these three questions, only the first one directly pertains to the overarching concept of

---

[13] In his elucidation of equity, Thomas underscores that in such circumstances, individuals are morally obligated to adhere to the precepts of natural law rather than those of conventional law. This philosophical underpinning, as articulated by Thomas, serves as the foundational basis of equity.

[14] The primary scholarly work dedicated to the examination of Radulphus Brito's philosophy and his commentary on Aristotle's *Ethics* is Costa 2008. For further insights into his life, one may refer to Deuffic 2002.

[15] Regarding this inquiry, one can refer to various contemporary studies as indicated at the outset of this chapter.

natural law, specifically articulated as follows: "Consequenter queritur utrum sit aliquod iustum naturale". The remaining two questions delve into specific topics, namely, the examination of the nature of sacrifice and the analysis of the natural union between male and female.[16] In his commentary on the general question, Radulphus's view aligns closely with that of Thomas.[17] In our discussion, we will concisely summarize the viewpoints shared with Thomas, while highlighting Radulphus's distinctive contributions. Additionally, we will briefly touch upon how the discussions concerning the two specific questions intersect with the broader theme of natural laws.

Radulphus defends the same opinion as Thomas in most of his commentary. He changed Thomas's exposition from a commentary on Aristotle's text to a scholastic question. but does not make major philosophical changes, or even additions. He describes conventional law as a specific implication of natural principles, but not a natural conclusion of these principles. He also summarizes Thomas's commentary on the different kinds of natural laws. Radulphus's main addition is the relation that he introduces between, on the one hand, the Aristotelian distinction between scientific and ethical learning made in the first book of the *Ethics*,

---

[16] "Consequenter queritur utrum sit aliquod iustum naturale; queritur utrum combinatio maris cum femella in ciuitate sit naturalis".

[17] Similar to other commentaries on Aristotle's *Ethics* labelled as "Averroist", Radulphus's commentary aligns with prevailing viewpoints on the majority of subjects, as is indicated in Costa's research.

and, on the other, the distinction between the way that natural specific law and conventional specific law derive from natural universal principles.

Et ideo male dicunt illi qui dicunt quod homines diu instructi in scientiis speculatiuis non possunt proficere in legibus: istud credo esse falsum, (tamen aliquis credit esse sufficienter instructus in scientiis speculatiuis et tamen non est) sed si non possint ibi proficere, hoc est quia ignorant modum procedendi debitum ibi, vnde Philosophus dat modum procedendi in scientiis legalibus: quia non est eodem modo procedendi in scientiis speculatiuis sicut in scientiis legalibus, nec equalis certitudo est vtrobique querenda; tamen illi qui sic sunt instructi in scientiis speculatiuis aduertentes ad modum procedendi quem dat ibi Philosophus, melius possunt ibi proficere quam alii.	And therefore, those who say that individuals who have been well-versed in speculative sciences cannot make progress in legal matters speak incorrectly: I believe this to be false, (although some may believe they are sufficiently versed in speculative sciences and yet are not), but if they cannot make progress there, it is because they are ignorant of the proper method of proceeding in that field. Hence, the philosopher provides a method of proceeding in legal sciences: for the process in speculative sciences is not the same as in legal sciences, nor is equal certainty sought in both; however, those who are well-versed in speculative sciences, paying attention to the method of proceeding prescribed by the Philosopher, can make better progress there than others.

At the outset of Aristotle's *Ethics*, Radulphus distinguishes between ethical and scientific learning; he extends this distinction to draw parallels between scientific and legal learning. While the methodologies of learning differ, they are not entirely separate. In speculative learning, the process of deriving conclusions from principles is characterized by a degree of certainty — an attribute absent in legal (and ethical) science. However, Radulphus claims that individuals well-versed in speculative science, who comprehend the method of drawing conclusions within that realm, are better equipped to render sound legal judgments than those lacking such knowledge.

A noteworthy addition made by Radulphus is his theoretical explication of the errors humans can commit when making legal decisions. Thomas acknowledges the existence of human errors in legal matters; Radulphus develops this by establishing a connection between ethics and legal decision-making. He asserts that the certainty attainable in speculative science cannot be replicated in legal inquiries, given the inherent link between legal and ethical questions. While Radulphus' insight represents a development, it is highly likely that Thomas would concur with this view, as it does not fundamentally alter Thomas's philosophical stance.

Towards the conclusion of his exposition, Radulphus establishes a connection between his explanation and Thomas's view that entirely natural things may not be right in all specific human situations.

The two subsequent questions within Radulphus' commentary delve into specific implications derived from these overarching principles. Radulphus elucidates that sacrifices possess a natural quality, yet the precise quantity of animals to be sacrificed remains a matter of convention. In the second question, Radulphus asserts that the union between man and woman is inherently natural, as it is indispensable for the preservation of humanity. He further expounds that the well-being of offspring necessitates the presence of both a father and a mother.

In Radulphus' commentary, we discern the profound influence exerted by Thomas's commentary on subsequent Latin commentators. Radulphus does not alter Thomas's perspectives but rather introduces certain distinctions that the Angelic Doctor would likely find acceptable.

Geraldus Odonis

Geraldus Odonis (c.1285-1351) was a Franciscan from the southern region of France, known for his teaching positions in Toulouse and Paris.[18] In question 13 of his commentary of the Ethics, Geraldus's interpretation of Aristotle closely mirrors that of Thomas. However, in question 16, he delves into the subject of natural law and introduces distinctions between various categories of natural and conventional laws.[19] As question 13 is the one

---

[18] I extend my gratitude to Robert Andrew for providing the transcription of the pertinent excerpts from Geraldus Odonis' *Commentarius in Aristotelis ethicam*, from the Venice 1500 edition, book V, lecture 13.

[19] While we do not delve into this subject here, it is noteworthy to observe that Geraldus incorporates divine law as a category within natural law, a departure from the positions of Albert and Thomas. Geraldus classifies natural law into three categories: human as animal, human as rational, and human as subject to divine law. In contrast, Thomas and Albert introduce distinct, albeit differing, differentiations between divine and natural law, refraining from categorizing divine law as a subset of natural law.

directly related to the Aristotelian text, we shall focus our quotations solely on this particular question.[20]

Geraldus's commentary largely follows the primary developments set forth by Thomas Aquinas and does not introduce any substantial philosophical innovations to the Doctor Angelicus's commentary. Geraldus explicitly asserts that natural principles possess binding authority even in societies unaware of them—a viewpoint influenced more by Albertus Magnus than Thomas Aquinas.

Geraldus also embraces Thomas's fundamental view by positing that all conventional laws are grounded in natural principles. For instance, the act of honouring benefactors is deemed natural, but the specific way this honour is bestowed is subject to convention.

Furthermore, Geraldus agrees with Thomas's view that natural laws can undergo change, albeit infrequently, as exemplified in Plato's *Republic* by the example of the sword. Conversely, changes in conventional laws are inherent to their application, such as variations in measurement standards across different regions. According to both authors, conventional laws, serving as specific applications of natural principles, should adapt to the particular needs of each society. In contrast, natural laws

---

[20] Question 16 addresses the various categories of natural and legal laws — a subject that is particularly pertinent to the Latin tradition of commentators and has a weaker connection to the original Aristotelian text. A comprehensive comprehension of this topic would necessitate an in-depth analysis of Geraldus's entire body of commentary.

encompass specific applications but are only subject to alteration in exceptional and rare circumstances.[21]

The only differences between Geraldus and Thomas are that Geraldus's text does not explicitly indicate that changes within natural law, such as the potentiality for ambidexterity, are inherently negative. Likewise, Geraldus's text does not definitively assert whether a conventional law is universally superior across the entirety of the world. Geraldus's interpretation of the concluding passage within the Aristotelian text is characterized by ambiguity, akin to Aristotle's original text, and does not unmistakably align with the viewpoint that certain conventional laws possess inherent natural superiority over others. In these two respects, Geraldus diverges from the perspectives of Albert and Thomas. Geraldus refrains from overtly opposing prior Latin commentators but, through omission, shapes his commentary to adhere more closely to the original Aristotelian text.

As demonstrated in Geraldus's commentary, as well as in Radulphus's commentary, it becomes evident how deeply Thomas influenced subsequent medieval Latin commentaries.

Conclusion

In summary, the Latin commentators have crafted a distinct interpretation of the Aristotelian text, characterized by their delineation of various forms of natural and conventional law. This distinctive approach commences with Albert's commentary and is consistently

---

[21] Several of these issues are linked to the topic of equity raised by Geraldus in question 16.

upheld by subsequent Latin commentators. The primary differentiation centres on two categories of natural law: 1. law derived from the commonality between human and animal instincts, and 2. law arising from the natural culmination of human attributes, particularly human intellect. Thomas significantly contributes to the latter interpretation by defining conventional law as a specific application of natural principles. While Aristotle's text provides some illustrative examples, this distinction is not overtly evident in the original Aristotelian text. This interpretation, which had previously appeared in Averroes' commentary, gained prominence and acceptance largely due to Thomas's influence.[22]

Another prominent trend among the Latin commentators is the idea that certain conventional laws are superior to others. This viewpoint is shared by both Thomas and Albert, but not by Geraldus. It finds some support in the Aristotelian text, particularly in its earliest Latin translation. However, it should be noted that this interpretation is not an inherent necessity within Aristotle's original text.

---

[22] This particular interpretation is conspicuously absent in the Byzantine tradition of commentators, as well as in Albert's commentary. Furthermore, there is no discernible influence of this perspective on Jewish philosophers who lack exposure to Thomas's writings.

Texts of the Latin Commentators

Albertus Magnus[23]

I:

CAPUT III: *De justo politico et naturali.*

Politici autem justi in contrarium quidem duae sunt species, quamvis plures sint modi. Una quidem species naturale justum : alia autem justum legale. *Naturale* autem dicimus, quod simpliciter naturale est, nullam legalis justi habens admixtionem. *Legale* autem, quod simpliciter legale est, nihil habet admixtum. Naturale quidem justum est, quod ubique et apud omnes homines quantum ad sui principia in communi sigillatim accepta vel sumpta, eamdem habet potentiam ad obligandum, et quantum ad sui principia non consistit in videri vel non videri, sicut jus positivum quod positum est ex ratione utilitatis communis ex his quae videbantur sapientibus et plebibus vel principibus, qui rempublicam pro tempore gubernant, et secundum casus emergentes ad utilitatem reipublicae statuerunt quae videbantur esse convenientia, vel ad boni communis promotionem, et ad mali exclusionem vel temperamentum. Et hoc est quod dicit Tullius in fine primae *Rethoricae* sic :« Naturre jus est, quod non opinio genuit, sed innata quaedam jus inseruit. » Haec autem innata jus ex genere potest esse, et ex specie. Ex genere autem dupliciter, scilicet ex genere secundum se, vel genere secundum quod stat sub specie determinata. Sed si est ex genere secundum se: tunc non obligat per modum justi, eo quod justum aequale est: aequale autem

---

[23] *Opera omnia*, ed. Borgnet (Paris, 1891), vol. VII: *Ethica*, pp. 366-371.

secundum proportionem. Tale autem secundum rationem non potest esse. Animal enim genus secundum se sine ordine ad rationem acceptum, nihil rationis. Et idcirco ad quod obligat, per instinctum naturalem obligat et non per modum justi, et sicut dicitur de jure naturali esse conjunctio maris et foeminae, liberorum procreatio, et vis illatae repulsio. Omne enim aut pro sui esse pugnat conservando, et pro his quae ad conservationem esse ordinantur, quae tantum tria sunt, cibus scilicet, et nidus, et pullus : pro uxore enim generaliter pugnant animalia.

Naturale autem ex specie est, quod unicuique dictat ratio ex solis rationis principiis informata, et non ex his quae inquisitione vel discussione inventa sunt. Et hoc modo dicit Tullius, quod "de jure naturali sunt religio, pietas, gratia, vindicatio, observantia, et veritas." Ratio enim naturalis dictat deos esse verendos. Unde Tullius, "Religio est, quae superioris cujusdam naturae quam divinam vocant, curam cerimoniamque affert." Et sic dicitur, quod jus poli jus naturale est: sed hoc non potest esse verum, nisi uno modo, scilicet quod jus poli dicatur quod ad polum colendum ex sola obligat ratione. Omnia enim quae a diis dicta vel statuta sunt, de naturali justo esse non possunt : cum quaedam eorum et supra rationem sunt, quaedam autem praeter rationem valde, quaedam etiam contra rationem inveniuntur. Naturalis etiam ratio dictat parentes honorare. Unde Tuliius, « Pietas est, per quam sanguine conjunctis, patriae benevolis officium et diligens tribuitur cultus » Locus enim qui pro patria ponitur, generationis principium est quemadmodum et pater. Natura etiam ad speciei conjunctos dictat amice et secundum retributiones vivere: quia homo secundum naturam civile animai est. Civilitas enim sine communicatione vicissitudinis stare non potest. Quam speciem justi Tullius vocat *gratiam,* quam sic diflinit, « Gratia est in qua amicitiarum et officiorum alterius memoria et alterius remunerandi voluntas continetur. » Natura etiam dictat contrarium insurgens esse repellendum: et hoc etiam *vindicatio* vocatur. Unde Tullius, « Vindicatio est, per quam vis sive violentia et injuria, et omnino omne quod obscurum est, defendendo aut irascendo propulsatur. » Cum autem homo politicum animai sit, ratio hominis est de ordinatione urbanitatis, in qua quidam praestant, et quidam aequales sunt. In praestantibus autem divinius bonum est: et tale bonum respicit *observantiam.* Unde Tullius, « Observantia est, per quam homines aliqua dignitate antecedentes cultu quodam et honore dignantur » Ratio etiam naturalis de omni re dictat, quod unumquodque secundum quod est in veritate suae naturum, ita determinetur: et hoc justum vocatur *veritas.* Unde Tullius, « Veritas est, per quam immutata ea quae sunt ac ante fuerunt aut futura sunt, dicuntur vel determinantur. »

Istae ergo sunt sex species justi naturalis: vel ad auctorem naturae, sicut prima species: vel ad ordinata ad naturam, sicut ultima: vel adjuncta in natura secundum lineam rectam vel transversalem acceptae. Sed in natura dupliciter accipiuntur, scilicet secundum conjuncta in esse, vel conjuncta in specie. Adjuncta enim secundum esse, pietas est. Conjuncta autem in specie, dupliciter conjuncta sunt, scilicet secundum se, et secundum ordinem humani boni. Adjuncta secundum se, gratia est: adjuncta secundum ordinem humani honi, ohservantia est. Et omnes istae quinque species sunt ad bonum. Contra malum autem in omnibus his vindicatio est.

Cum ergo dicitur quod justum naturale verum habet eamdem potentiam, hoc intelligendum est quantum ad prima principia justi naturalis, et non quantum ad ea quae per studium vel discussionem ex talibus emergentibus eliciuntur. Hoc enim consuetudinis jus est, et non naturae. Unde Tullius, "Consuetudinis justitia est: quod aut leviter attractum a natura, et majus fecit usus, ut religionem quae multis institutis modo differt apud diversos, aut pietatem, aut quaecumque eorum quae praedicta sunt." Haec enim a natura profecta videmus crevisse, et variata esse per consuetudinem et responsa sapientium et statuta principum. Propter quod etiam in morem profecta sunt, vel vetustate, vel vulgi approbatione, aut per pactum, aut par, aut judicatum. Cum tamen prima principia apud omnes ejusdem sint potentiae. Aequaliter enim omnibus dictat ratio deos verendos, parentes honorandos, socialiter vivendum cum aequalibus, melioribus meliorem cultum impendendum, unumquodque sicut se habet esse determinandum, et contrarium esse repellendum.

Consuetudinis autem jus in videri et non videri sive opinari consistit, et tribus innititur, pacto scilicet, pari, et judicato. Pactum autem ad voluntatem communicantium refertur: par vero ad rei sive negotii requale, judicatum autem ad statutum. Unde Tullius, « Pactum est, quod inter aliquos convenit. Par autem, quod in omnes aequabile est (aequabile autem dicit secundum proportiones superius inductas). Judicatum autem, quod alicujus vel aliquorum sententiis jam constitutum est. »

Sicut autem diximus modo in communi de justo naturali, ita dicimus de omnibus partibus ejus. Deum enim unum esse propter religionem de justo naturali est. Non esse perjurandum, vel non esse falsum testimonium dicendum, de justo naturali est propter veritatem. Parentes autem honorandos de justo naturali est propter pietatem. Non esse moechandum vel furandum vel occidendum, de justo naturali est propter gratiam. Et sic in omnibus facile est videre: quia sicut divinius dicit Basilius, « Omnia principia naturalis juris in naturali judicatorio rationis descripta sunt. » Non aliter homo honesti esset particeps, nisi principia honesti essent in ipso per naturam: sicut nec scientiae particeps esset, si principia scibilium non essent in ipso, ut probat Aristoteles. Natura enim nihil facit ad aliquem actum, nisi omnia principia quae sunt ad illum actum et instrumenta conferat: aliter enim vanum sive frustra et deficere in necessariis esset in natura, quod secundum Peripateticos absurdum est.

Sic ergo intelligitur quod justum naturale ubique eamdem habet potentiam et quod non consistit in videri vel non videri. Potentiam autem dicimus, primam inclinationem ex natura rationali, et non illam quae accipitur in effectu. Quamvis enim apud Trivallos pium sit interficere parentes, tamen hoc non dictat natura de parente secundum quod parens est: sed ad hoc mala consuetudo provexit ex ratione male arguens, scilicet quod magis pium sit parentem miserum miseriam cito finire, quam in miseria diu vivere. Unde etiam apud abutentes jure naturali prima principia ejusdem potentiae sunt, cujus sunt apud bene utentes. Et ideo imperfectum est dictum Eustratii et Michaelis Ephesii, qui dicunt justum naturale non esse ejusdem potentiae, nisi apud bene utentes ipso secundum naturam. Apud bestialiter autem viventes, nullam dicunt esse potentiam justi naturalis. Homo enim quamdiu homo est, principiis humanis non destituitur.

Legale autem justum quod pure legale est et simpliciter, est illud quod ex principio secundum se acceptum, nihil differt utrum sit vel aliter fiat, ita scilicet quod sic faciens nec laudatur nec vituperatur, et aliter faciens similiter. Quando autem ponitur per institutionem principis vel plebis, multum differt propter institutionem: sic enim faciens ut institutum est, praemiatur: aliter autem faciens, punitur. Verbi gratia, sicut est mina redimi captivos, et non amplius, hoc in bello Atheniensium et Lacedaemoniorum ad invicem pari consensu utrorumque statutum est: unde post bellum Lacedaemonii ad Athenas miserunt Metellum et Endicum et Philoloculum legatos, qui captivos mina redemerunt et ultra non dederunt, sicut refert Androchion historiographus: et sicut est capram sacrificare et non duas oves: et generalìter loquendo quaecumque in singularibus operationibus sola lege ponuntur: et quia institutione sola potentiam habent obligandi, sicut verbi gratia quod apud Amphipolim institutum est Brasidae sacrificare, quae ante inter deos non habebat venerationem: et sicut sunt sententialia, quae propter hoc solum habent vigorem, quia per sententiam judicis determinata sunt. Haec autem ideo legalia dicuntur, quia ex natura nullam habent potentiam et omnem accipiunt ex lege, secundum quod Tullius dicit de lege, quod « legis jus est, quod in eo scripta quod populo expositum est ut observet, continetur. » Sic enim legale jus valde stricte sumitur, pro eo scilicet quod nullum nisi ex lege habet vigorem.

Ex his patet quod consuetudinis medium est inter legale et naturale, scilicet quod a natura profectum, lege sancitum est, secundum quod lex large sumitur sic diffinita, « Lex est jus scriptum praecipiens honestum, prohibens contrarium. » Sive enim scriptum sit in natura, sive in determinatione construentium, sive in approbatione consuetudinis secundum aliquem modum legis habet approbationem.

II & III:
CAPUT IV: *De errore quorumdam quj justum naturale non unius apud omnes determinant.*

Quibusdam autem videtur quod omnia justa sint legalia, et nullam nisi ex institione vim habentia. De naturalibus dicunt quod omne naturale immobile sit, et quod ubique habeant eamdem potentiam, quemadmodum ignis et hic et in Persis ardet secundum ustivam potentiam quae est in ipso. Sed justa non dicunt esse naturalia: eo quod omnia justa mota esse conspiciunt, et (sicut dicimus in primo hujus scientiae libro) tantam habent diversitatem et errorem, quod lege posita esse videntur et non natura. Hi tamen decepti sunt. Non enim sic se habet: sed potius quodammodo naturalia immutabilia sunt, scilicet quantum ad prima principia quibus homo ad bonum et ad verum ordinatur: haec enim humanitati inscripta sunt, et non mutantur. Usus autem horum relatus ad operationes, in multas variatur consuetudines et institutiones. Unde quamvis apud deos omne justum nequaquam aliter se habeat, eo quod nihil diis mutabile est: apud nos autem natura ens aliquo modo mutabile est, quia omne quod in natura humana est, mutabile est: et quamvis hoc sit, tamen humanorum justorum aliquod est naturale, aliquod non naturale.

Inter ea autem quae natura sunt, quale sit illud justum quod cum natura sit, convenit tamen aliter se habere: et quale sit illud justum quod non natura est, sed est legale: et compositio quaedam quae convenit inter homines quod etiam mobile est contingens aliter se habere: et utrum ambo ista similiter mobilia sint, manifestum ex praeinductis est.

Et in aliis qure praeinduci possunt, eadem congruet determinatio. In membris enim animalium, quamvis una position naturalis sit, tamen natura in diversitate materiae operans, aliquando variat ordinem. Quamvis enim omne animal ex dextro et sinistro componatur, tamen in animalibus inveniuntur ambo dextra: et quamvis hepar in dextro sit et splen in sinistro, tamen·conversus modus saepe invenitur. Et hujus causa est, quia tanta fuit inaequalitas materiae, quod natura ordinem debitum adhibere non potuit: et ne totum per confusionem perderetur, fecit quod potuit, aliquod malum tolerans: et sic provehens materiam ad proximum quod potuit, duxit naturae ordinem. Quod in omnibus urbanitatibus oportet observari: quia quaecumque de numero sunt inventa secundum compositionem quae est inter homines, et secundum id quod confert reipublicae, illa similia sunt mensuris. Mensuris autem diversa similiter mensurari non possunt: eo quod una mensura non uno modo potest eis applicari, sicut in curvis et rectis et in nodosis et planis: cum tamen hoc necesse sit ad unam mensuram referri. Sic non est ubique aequalis vini et frumenti mensura: sed uhi haec abundant et venduntur pro copia, minor mensura datur: ubi autem ista venduntur et emuntur pro necessitate, et ubi abundant minus, ibi eodem pretio minor mensura venditur quo major in loco copiae emebatur. Sic etiam naturalia justa pro diversitate cohabitantium necesse est variari. Hominum enim tanta diversitas est, quod ad unum ordinem justi naturalis quem in usu in omni opere suo participet, reduci non potest. Non tamen propter hoc a regimine abstinendum: quia si non potest reduci in ordinem primum et principalem, reducitur tamen ad aliquem qui circa primum est, et ad primum habet respectum.

Similiter et illa justa quae non naturalia sunt, sed humana, vel legalia, non eadem ubique sunt: quia neque una et eadem urbanitas est apud omnes. Sed hoc verum est, quod illa omnium quae urbanitatum secundum naturam optima est, una sola est et ubique, ad quam omnes aliae habent respectum: illam tamen observatam fuisse in communitate in toto sine omnis naturalis justi variatione non memini me legisse, nisi primo apud Zebadaeos et secundo apud Bragmanos. Unde Didymus Bragmanorum rex leges edidit. Unam quidem, mulieres non uti decore quem natura negavit. Aliam autem, non aedificandas domus esse: eo quod antra dum vivunt perficiunt hospitium, et dum moriuntur, in sepulcrum. Tertiam, non esse venandum: quia cui natura fugam dedit, dum fugit, non est insequendum. Et alias multas tales quae in libro Didymi quem Alexandro scripsit, continentur.

Justorum autem legalium omnium sive naturalia sint, sive legalia sive consuetudinalia unumquodque sic se habet ut universale ad particularia. Universale enim in multis et de multis est secundum rationem non variatum, et sic est de multis: et cum multa sint in quibus est magnam et multimodam secundum esse habet variationem. Per omnem eumdem modum est in his quae justa sunt, quae sunt mensura operum nostrorum. Operata enim ab hominibus valde multa et differentia sunt; Justorum autem sive naturalium sive legalium quod mensura operatum est, unumquodque est unum secundum se et rationem. Sic enim mensurando universale est, et de multis secundum quod ponitur in usu, non omnia sibi aequaliter applicabilia invenit: et ideo in usu necesse est variari, qui a sic non de multis, sed in multis est.

Thomas Aquinas[24]

[73720] *Sententia Ethic.*, lib. 5 lect. 12 n. 1 Postquam philosophus ostendit quale sit politicum iustum, quod est simpliciter iustum, hic ponit divisionem huius iusti politici. Et primo dividit iustum politicum in species. Secundo tangit divisionem huius iusti in individua, ibi, iustorum autem, et legalium et cetera. Circa primum tria facit. Primo proponit divisionem. Secundo exponit eam, ibi, naturale quidem et cetera. Tertio excludit errorem contra divisionem praedictam, ibi: videtur autem quibusdam et cetera. Dicit ergo primo, quod politicum iustum dividitur in duo: quorum unum est iustum naturale, aliud autem iustum legale. Est autem haec eadem divisio cum divisione quam iuristae ponunt, quod iuris aliud est naturale, aliud est positivum; idem enim nominant illi ius quod Aristotiles iustum, nam et Isidorus dicit in libro Etymologiarum, quod ius dicitur quasi iustum. Videtur autem esse contrarietas quantum ad hoc, quod politicum idem est quod civile; et sic id quod apud philosophum ponitur ut divisum, apud iuristas videtur poni ut dividens, nam ius civile ponunt partem iuris positivi.

[73721] *Sententia Ethic.*, lib. 5 lect. 12 n. 2 Sed attendendum est, quod aliter sumitur politicum vel civile hic apud philosophum et aliter apud iuristas; philosophus enim hic nominat politicum iustum vel civile ex usu, quo scilicet cives utuntur; iuristae autem nominant ius politicum vel civile ex causa, quod scilicet civitas aliqua sibi constituit, et ideo convenienter hic a

---

[24] Based on the text of the *Opera omnia* provided in the Corpus thomisticum: *Ethica*, liber V, lectio XII.

philosopho nominatur *legale*, idest lege positum, quod et illi dicunt positivum; convenienter autem per haec duo dividitur iustum politicum, utuntur enim cives iusto et eo quod natura menti humanae indidit, et eo quod est positum lege.

[73722] *Sententia Ethic.*, lib. 5 lect. 12 n. 3 Deinde cum dicit: naturale quidem etc., manifestat membra divisionis praemissae. Et primo manifestat iustum naturale dupliciter. Uno modo secundum effectum vel virtutem, dicens quod iustum naturale est quod habet ubique eandem potentiam, id est virtutem, ad inducendum ad bonum et ad arcendum a malo. Quod quidem contingit eo quod natura, quae est causa huius iusti, eadem est ubique apud omnes, iustum vero quod est ex positione alicuius civitatis vel principis apud illos tantum est virtuosum, qui subduntur iurisdictioni illius civitatis vel principis. Alio modo manifestat hoc iustum secundum causam, cum dicit, quod iustum naturale non consistit *in videri vel non videri*, idest non oritur ex aliqua opinione humana, sed ex natura. Sicut enim in speculativis sunt quaedam naturaliter cognita, ut principia indemonstrabilia et quae sunt propinqua his; quaedam vero studio hominum adinventa, ita etiam in operativis sunt quaedam principia naturaliter cognita quasi indemonstrabilia principia et propinqua his, ut malum esse vitandum, nulli esse iniuste nocendum, non esse furandum et similia, alia vero sunt per industriam hominum excogitata, quae dicuntur hic iusta legalia.

[73723] *Sententia Ethic.*, lib. 5 lect. 12 n. 4 Est autem considerandum, quod iustum naturale est ad quod hominem natura inclinat. Attenditur autem in homine duplex natura. Una quidem, secundum quod est animal, quae est sibi aliisque animalibus communis; alia

autem est natura hominis quae est propria sibi inquantum est homo, prout scilicet secundum rationem discernit turpe et honestum. Iuristae autem illud tantum dicunt ius naturale, quod consequitur inclinationem naturae communis homini et aliis animalibus, sicut coniunctio maris et feminae, educatio natorum, et alia huiusmodi. Illud autem ius, quod consequitur propriam inclinationem naturae humanae, inquantum scilicet homo est rationale animal, vocant ius gentium, quia eo omnes gentes utuntur, sicut quod pacta sint servanda, quod legati etiam apud hostes sint tuti, et alia huiusmodi. Utrumque autem horum comprehenditur sub iusto naturali, prout hic a philosopho accipitur.

[73724] *Sententia Ethic.*, lib. 5 lect. 12 n. 5 Secundo ibi: legale autem etc., manifestat iustum legale. Et videtur ponere tres differentias huius iusti. Quarum prima est: cum universaliter vel communiter aliquid lege ponitur; et quantum ad hoc dicit quod legale iustum dicitur quod *ex principio quidem*, scilicet antequam lege statuatur, nihil differt utrum sic vel aliter fiat: sed *quando iam ponitur*, idest statuitur lege, tunc differt, quia hoc servare est iustum, praeterire iniustum. Sicut in aliqua civitate statutum est quod captivus redimatur mna, quocumque scilicet certo pretio, et quod sacrificetur capra, non autem quod sacrificentur duae oves.

[73725] *Sententia Ethic.*, lib. 5 lect. 12 n. 6 Alia vero differentia iusti legalis est, secundum quod aliquid lege statuitur in aliquo singulari; puta cum civitas vel princeps alicui personae concedit aliquod privilegium, quod dicitur lex privata. Et quantum ad hoc dicit: quod adhuc sunt iusta legalia, non solum illa quae communiter statuuntur, sed quaecumque homines ponunt pro lege in aliquibus singularibus; sicut in quadam civitate statutum

est quod sacrificetur cuidam mulieri, nomine Brasidae, quae magnam utilitatem civitati attulerat.

[73726] *Sententia Ethic.*, lib. 5 lect. 12 n. 7 Tertia differentia iusti legalis est, prout sententiae a iudicibus datae dicuntur quaedam iusta legalia. Et quantum ad hoc subdit, quod etiam sententialia sunt iusta legalia.

[73727] *Sententia Ethic.*, lib. 5 lect. 12 n. 8 Est autem hic considerandum, quod iustum legale sive positivum oritur semper a naturali, ut Tullius dicit in sua rhetorica. Dupliciter tamen aliquid potest oriri a iure naturali. Uno modo sicut conclusio ex principiis; et sic ius positivum vel legale non potest oriri a iure naturali; praemissis enim existentibus, necesse est conclusionem esse; sed cum iustum naturale sit semper et ubique, ut dictum est, hoc non competit iusto legali vel positivo. Et ideo necesse est quod quicquid ex iusto naturali sequitur, quasi conclusio, sit iustum naturale; sicut ex hoc quod est nulli esse iniuste nocendum, sequitur non esse furandum, quod item ad ius naturale pertinet. Alio modo oritur aliquid ex iusto naturali per modum determinationis; et sic omnia iusta positiva vel legalia ex iusto naturali oriuntur. Sicut furem esse puniendum est iustum naturale, sed quod sit etiam puniendum tali vel tali poena, hoc est lege positum.

[73728] *Sententia Ethic.*, lib. 5 lect. 12 n. 9 Attendendum est etiam quod iustum legale dupliciter oritur a naturali secundum modum praedictum. Uno modo cum permixtione. Alio modo sine permixtione alicuius humani erroris, et hoc etiam exempla Aristotilis demonstrant; naturaliter enim iustum est quod civi non ob suam culpam oppresso subveniatur et per consequens quod captivus redimatur: taxatio autem pretii, quae

pertinet ad iustum legale, procedit ex praedicto iusto naturali absque omni errore. Est etiam naturale iustum quod benefactori honor exhibeatur; sed quod honor divinus exhibeatur homini est ex errore humano et tale est quod sacrificetur Brasidae. Sententialia vero iusta sunt applicationes iustorum legalium ad particularia facta.

I.

[73729] *Sententia Ethic.*, lib. 5 lect. 12 n. 10 Deinde cum dicit: videtur autem etc., excludit errorem contra praedictam divisionem. Et circa hoc tria facit. Primo proponit errorem cum sua ratione. Secundo solvit, ibi, hoc autem non est et cetera. Tertio movet quamdam quaestionem ex solutione ortam. Dicit ergo primo quod quibusdam visum est quod omnia iusta sint *talia*, scilicet lege posita, ita quod nihil sit iustum naturale. Quae quidem fuit opinio Cirenaeorum, sectatorum Aristipi Socratici. Et movebantur tali ratione: quia illud quod est secundum naturam est immobile et ubicumque sit habet eamdem virtutem, (sicut patet de igne qui ardet et in Graecia et in Perside, quod non videtur esse verum circa iusta, quia omnia iusta videntur aliquando esse mota. Nihil enim videtur esse magis iustum quam quod deponenti depositum reddatur; et tamen non est reddendum depositum furioso reposcenti gladium vel proditori patriae reposcenti pecunias ad arma: sic ergo videtur quod nulla sint naturaliter iusta.

[73730] *Sententia Ethic.*, lib. 5 lect. 12 n. 11 Deinde cum dicit: hoc autem non est etc., ponit solutionem. Et dicit quod id quod dictum est quod naturalia sint immobilia, non ita se habet universaliter, sed aliquo modo est verum; quia natura rerum divinarum nequaquam aliter se habet, puta substantiarum

separatarum et caelestium corporum, quae antiqui deos vocabant; sed apud nos homines, qui inter res corruptibiles sumus, est aliquid quidem secundum naturam, et tamen quicquid est in nobis est mutabile vel per se vel per accidens. Nihilominus tamen est in nobis aliquid naturale sicut habere pedes, et aliquid non naturale, sicut habere tunicam, et sic etiam, licet omnia quae sunt apud nos iusta aliqualiter moveantur, nihilominus tamen quaedam eorum sunt naturaliter iusta.

II.

[73731] *Sententia Ethic.*, lib. 5 lect. 12 n. 12 Deinde cum dicit: quale autem natura etc., movet quamdam dubitationem ex praecedenti solutione exortam. Et circa hoc duo facit: primo proponit quaestionem; secundo solvit, ibi: manifestum et in aliis et cetera. Primo igitur proponit talem quaestionem. Si enim omnia iusta humana mobilia sunt, restat quaestio, inter ea quae contingunt aliter se habere, quale sit iustum secundum naturam, et quale non secundum naturam, sed secundum legis positionem et ad placitum hominum, ex quo ambo sunt similiter mobilia.

[73732] *Sententia Ethic.*, lib. 5 lect. 12 n. 13 Deinde cum dicit manifestum et in aliis etc., solvit praedictam quaestionem. Et circa hoc duo facit. Primo ostendit qualiter iusta naturalia sint mobilia. Secundo qualiter iusta legalia, ibi, quae autem secundum compositionem et cetera. Dicit ergo primo manifestum esse quod etiam in aliis naturalibus quae sunt apud nos eadem determinatio congruit sicut et in naturaliter iustis. Ea enim quae sunt naturalia apud nos sunt quidem eodem modo ut in pluribus, sed ut in paucioribus deficiunt; sicut naturale est quod pars dextra sit vigorosior

quam sinistra, et hoc in pluribus habet veritatem; et tamen contingit ut in paucioribus aliquos fieri ambidextros, qui sinistram manum habent ita valentem ut dextram: ita etiam et ea quae sunt naturaliter iusta, utputa depositum esse reddendum, ut in pluribus est observandum, sed ut in paucioribus mutatur.

[73733] *Sententia Ethic.*, lib. 5 lect. 12 n. 14 Est tamen attendendum quod quia rationes etiam mutabilium sunt immutabiles, si quid est nobis naturale quasi pertinens ad ipsam hominis rationem, nullo modo mutatur, puta hominem esse animal. Quae autem consequuntur naturam, puta dispositiones, actiones et motus mutantur ut in paucioribus. Et similiter etiam illa quae pertinent ad ipsam iustitiae rationem nullo modo possunt mutari, puta non esse furandum, quod est iniustum facere. Illa vero quae consequuntur, mutantur ut in minori parte.

[73734] *Sententia Ethic.*, lib. 5 lect. 12 n. 15 Deinde cum dicit: quae autem secundum compositionem etc., ostendit qualiter iusta legalia sunt mutabilia indifferenter. Et dicit quod illa quae sunt iusta *secundum compositionem et conferens*, idest secundum quod est condictum inter homines propter aliquam utilitatem, sunt similia mensuris rerum venalium, puta vini et frumenti. (Non enim sunt ubique aequales mensurae vini et frumenti,) sed ubi emuntur propter maiorem copiam sunt maiores, ubi autem venduntur propter minorem copiam sunt minores. Ita etiam iusta quae non sunt naturalia, sed per homines posita, non sunt eadem ubique, sicut non ubique eadem poena imponitur furi. Et huius ratio est, quia non est eadem ubique urbanitas sive politia. Omnes enim leges ponuntur secundum quod

congruit fini politiae, sed tamen sola una est optima politia secundum naturam ubicumque sit.

Radulphus Brito[25]

> *Consequenter queritur vtrum sit aliquod iustum naturale.*
> *Arguitur quod non.*

<1>
Quia illud non est naturale quod non manet idem apud omnes; sed nullum iustum manet idem apud omnes; ideo etc. Maior patet: quia naturalia sunt eadem apud omnes. Minor declaratur: quia quodcumque iustum quod dicitur naturale, sicut vnicuique reddere suum depositum, istum iustum videtur maxime naturale, et tamen istud in omnibus non est seruandum, quia furioso deponenti gladium non est reddendus gladius.

<2>
Item. Iustum habet esse in communicatione hominum; sed nulla communicatio hominum est naturalis; quare etc. Maior patet: quia omne iustum ordinatur ad communicationem humanam. Minor de se patet: quia omnis communicatio humana est ex voluntate et constitutione humana.

In oppositum est Philosophus in illa parte: Politici autem..., vbi distinguit ius naturale et positiuum. Intelligendum est quod quoddam est ius naturale et

---

[25] *Quaestiones in Aristotelis libros ethicorum,* edited by Iacopo Costa, Introduction (in Italian) and critical text. Studia artistarum 16, Turnhout: Brepols, 2008, pp.459-462.

quoddam ius positiuum. Propter quod est notandum quod sicut in speculatiuis sunt quedam principia prima que naturaliter ab omnibus cognoscuntur sic [intelligendo] quod cognitis suis terminis intellectus speculatiuus statim eis assentit, ita etiam in agibilibus et practicis sunt quedam principia agibilius quibus intellectus practicus statim assentit, sicut sunt ista: non est faciendum malum nec est fugiendum bonum nec alteri sponte nocendum et sic de aliis: istis statim intellectus practicus assentit; modo ista principia quibus sic intellectus practicus assentit dicuntur iura naturalia, quia illud dicitur ius naturale ad quod intellectus cuiuslibet bene dispositus assentit; modo intellectus cuiuslibet bene dispositus istis principiis assentit (sicut 'malum est fugiendum' et consimilibus: quilibet enim ista concedit); ideo ista dicuntur ius naturale.

Sed est intelligendum quod ius naturale, quod dicitur a Philosopho ius naturale, distingunt iuriste in ius gentium et ius naturale, quia duplex est natura humana, scilicet vna vnde animal est et alia vnde homo et rationalis; modo illud iustum quod inest hominibus vnde animalia vocatur a iuristis ius naturale, sicut quod mulier cum viro coniugatur ad generationem prolis, istud est ius naturale et istud inest homini vnde animal, et quod fiat educatio vel nutritio puerorum, istud est ius naturale et inest etiam homini vnde animal, quia i stud aliis animalibus inest. Aliud [etiam] est ius quod Philosophus vocat naturale et iuriste vocant ius gentium, et istud ius est quod inest homini vnde homo et non vnde animal est, sicut quod amicis et benefactoribus sit benefaciendum et malefactoribus et inimicis malefaciendum, istud vocant ius gentium, et quod legati vel nuntii apud hostes sint securi: hoc est ius naturale homini vnde homo, et ista iura apud omnes homines seruantur; et Philosophus comprehendit vtrumque sub iure naturali, iuriste autem distingunt ipsum in ius naturale et ius gentium, vt dictum est.

Aliud est ius positiuum vel legale, et istum est deriuatum a iure naturali non sicut conclusio deriuatur a premissis: quia sicut ex premissis necessariis non sequitur nisi conclusio necessaria, ita etiam ex premissis que sunt iuste iustitia naturali sequitur conclusio iusta naturaliter, sicut: non est nocendum iniuste alteri, sed furari est iniuste nocere alteri, ergo non est furandum: ista conclusio est ius naturale sicut premisse. Sic ergo ius positiuum non est deriuatum a iure naturali sicut conlusio a premissis, sed magis per modum cuiusdam determinationis et contractionis: sicut ius naturale dicit quod diis est sacrificandum, sed quod sic vel sic sit diis sacrificandum, hoc est ius positiuum, et sic per modum contractionis deriuatur a iure naturali. Etiam ius naturale est vnumquemque iniuste operantem punire, quod tamen tali pena puniatur, vt incisione auris vel capitis vel suspensione istud est ius positiuum; et ideo omnes leges positiue fundate sunt super aliquam rationem naturalem. Et ideo male dicunt illi qui dicunt quod homines diu instructi in scientiis speculatiuis non possunt proficere in legibus: istud credo esse falsum, [tamen aliquis credit esse sufficienter instructus in scientiis speculatiuis et tamen non est] sed si non possint ibi proficere, hoc est quia ignorant modum procedendi debitum ibi, vnde Philosophus dat modum procedendi in scientiis legalibus: quia non est eodem modo procedendi in scientiis speculatiuis sicut in scientiis legalibus, nec equalis certitudo est vtrobique querenda; tamen illi qui sic sunt instructi in scientiis speculatiuis aduertentes ad modum procedendi quem dat ibi Philosophus, melius possunt ibi proficere quam alii.

Tunc ad rationes. Ad primam. Cum dicitur: illud non est naturale quod non manet idem apud omnes, quia naturalia manent eadem apud omnes, dico quod verum est quod naturalia manent eadem apud omnes vt in pluribus, vnde opera naturalia non semper manent eodem modo apud omnes. Et cum dicitur: iustum non manet idem apud omnes, dico quod istud raro accidit et in casu particulari; modo non est inconueniens naturalia deficere raro.

Ad aliam. Iustum habet esse in communicatione hominum, concedo. Et cum dicitur: communicatio hominum non est naturalis, falsum est, quia I Politicorum dicitur quod homo est animal naturaliter politicum et ciuile siue communicatiuum, et ideo communicatio est naturalis; tamen quod sic communicent, hoc est ex voluntate et institutione humana; tamen quod absolute communicent, hoc non est ex voluntate.

Geraldus Odonis

1.

Supra egit de separando iure politico a dominativo et paterno (1134b8), hic autem agit de iure politico naturali et positivo. Primo autem secundum sententiam proprium ius dividit. Secundo secundum aliorum sententiam contra suam divisionem abiicit, ibi: Videtur autem quibusdam (1134b25). Tertio obiectionem solvit, ibi: Hic autem non est sic (1134b26). Quarto iterum contra sequendam dubitationem movet, ibi: *Quare autem natura* (1134b36). Quinto illam dubitationem removet, ibi: *Manifestum etiam* (1134b32).

2.

Dicit (1134b18) ergo primo quod iusti vel iuris politici duae sunt species. Quandoque hoc ius politicum est naturale vim habens, non a lege sed a natura. Aliud autem ius politicum est legale vim habens, non a natura sed a lege.

3.

Deinde exponit huius divisionis membra, describens utrumque ius. Et dicit quod ius naturale est quod ubique habet eandem vim et potentiam. "Naturalia enim sunt eadem apud omnes," ut primo Perihermenias habetur. |Y f. 109rb| Et ius naturale est quod non habet vim et potentiam ex hoc quod est videri istis vel non videri istis, sed aliis. Sed habet etiam vim et potentiam ante videri sicut ius honorandi parentes vim obligandi habet antequam homo consideret; immo dato quod non videretur homini quod deberet honorare parentes, ipse tamen remanet obligatus semper ad hoc, et peccat si non honoret. Nec ignorantia negotialis vel dispositionis excusat.

4.

Deinde (1134b19) de iure legali dicit quod ius legale est illud quod ex principio ante legis positionem nichil differt vel sic vel aliter agere, quia per naturam non est praedeterminatum quod hoc sit bonum vel malum, quod sit faciendum vel fugiendum. Sed quando ius per legem vel per consuetudinem ponitur vel est iam positum, differet multum. Quia obedire bonum est, et praeterire malum – puta redimere captivum praetio unius mnae, id est, duarum librarum cum dimidia; vel quod capra sacrificetur plus deo quam duae oves. Vel adhuc in singularibus privilegiis aliquarum personarum cum ipsa privilegia ponuntur in lege, puta cum domina Brasida vel Braida fuit privilegiata ob merita suae ingentissimae |X im431b| probitatis quod sacrificaretur ei. Et iterum iura legalis et positiva sunt iudicia sententialia seu sententiae a recta data per iudices et arbitros vel aliorum quorum interest iudicare.

5.

Est autem sciendum quod in hiis exemplis Philosophi sunt aliqua de iure naturali, aliqua vero de legali et positivo. Quoniam omne ius positivum statuitur ad deserviendum et famulandum iuri naturae. Quare unumquodque praeceptum iuris positivi praesupponit aliquod praeceptum iuris naturalis cui famulatur et deservit. Et ideo in hiis omnibus exemplis tangitur aliquid de utroque. Verbi gratia, redemptio captivorum est de naturali iure quod vocatur 'pietas'. Sed quod redemptio fiat per hoc pretium quod est mna, hoc est simpliciter positivum. Item, quod sacrificetur deo corporaliter vel spiritualiter, hoc est de iure naturali quod vocatur 'religio'. Sed quod sacrificatur ei capra plus quam ovis, hoc est simpliciter positivum.

6.

Item, quod illi Braside fiat honor et remuneratio, hoc est de iure naturali, quod vocatur 'gratia' vel 'gratitudo', per quam sumus benefici et benivoli benefactoribus nostris.

Sed illi Braside sacrificetur tamquam deo, hoc est de iure simpliciter falso nequam et iniquo per humanam insipientiam posito. Unde in casu isto ius positivum, intendens deservire et obsequi iuri naturali, non servit ei sed contradicit ei. Quia ius naturale prohibet honorem divinum tribuere creaturae. Honor autem sacrificiorum debetur soli deo.

7.

Item, quod veritas sententiarum teneatur ut iusta, hoc est de iure naturali quod vocatur 'veritas'. Sed quod teneat sententia huius arbitrii, vel ius huius iudicis, vel ius, hoc est simpliciter positivum. De hoc autem quattuor iure naturali habes supra eodem capitulo 2, quaestione prima.

8.

Consequenter ibi: Videtur autem (1134b24), contra praemissam divisionem obiicit secundum aliorum sententiam, dicens quod quibusdam videtur quod omnia iura sunt talia, id est, positiva et non naturalia, contra praedictam divisionem. Quorum ratio est quia omne quod est per naturam est immobile, et eandem vim, et eandem habet potentiam apud omnes et ubique, quemadmodum ignis de iure suo et ex vi sua; et hoc in Graecia |X im432a| et in terra Persarum ardet. Sed omnia iura et iusta conspicimus esse mota, non immobilia. Nihil enim potest esse amplius de iure naturali quam quod sit "communis omnium possessio," ut in Decretis distinctione prima, capitulo ius. Et tamen istud est amotum universaliter ab hominibus. Videmus enim in particularibus casibus non observari generalia iuris naturalis praecepta, puta quod depositum est reddendum ei qui deposuit, si deposcat. Si autem aliquis gladium deposuerit, et furiosus factus deposcat, gladium non est ei reddendum – etiam de iure. Quare videtur nullum ius sit simpliciter naturale, sed omnia sicut positiva eo quod omnia sunt mobilia.

9.

Consequenter ibi: Hic autem non est sic (1134b25), praemissam obiectionem solvit, dicens quod maior propositio dictae rationis est falsa, quia ius naturale non est sic se habens, quod scilicet sit universaliter immobile; quia quamvis apud deos apud quos Plato astruit esse iura nequaquam sit aliquid mobile vel aliter et aliter se habens; tamen apud nos est aliquid a natura, quod est naturale; et cum hoc est mobile. Quia certe totum et omne quod est apud homines est |Y f. 109va| aliqualiter mobile. Et ideo ad mutationem hominis, sicut dicebatur de furioso, debet mutari ius circa hominem. Et tamen utrumque ius naturale, puta quod gladius reddatur et non reddatur ei cuius est, quia utrumque fit in favorem eius. Debet enim ei reddi ad bonum et non debet ei ad malum. Et propter hoc adhuc stat prima divisio iuris, quod ius humanum hoc quidem est a natura, puta ius naturale; aliud autem non est a natura, puta legale.

10.

Consequenter ibi: Quare autem (1134b30). Item contra se dubium removet, dicens quod si ambo iura, naturale scilicet et legale, sunt mobilia, rationabiliter dubitatur quare ius de numero istorum contingentium iurium et aliter se habere possibilium erit a natura, id est per naturam et naturale, et quale non erit naturale sed legale, et quaedam humana compositio, quia non apparet ratio huius diversitatis.

11.

Consequenter ibi: Manifestum (1134b32), istud dubium removet, dicens manifestum esse quod etiam in aliis eadem determinatio et eadem ratio congruit, in quibus posset eadem |X im432b| dubitatione apparere sicut apparet de dextra et sinistra, quia naturaliter dextra est melior quam sinistra et aptior ad operandum; et tamen aliquando contingit aliquos homines fieri ambidextros, et nullam differentiam esse inter istam et illam. Et aliquando contingit quod sinistra est aptior quam dextra. Et ideo ius naturale non differt a legali, per hoc quod est numquam moveri.

12.

Differt igitur aliter, quia iustorum illa quae sunt secundum humanam compositionem et secundum conferens seu commodum communitati, vel principi, vel alicui homini proveniens quae sunt simpliciter iura positiva, illa in quam sunt similia mensuris quae non ubique sunt aequales, puta mensurae frumenti et vini, quae ubi emuntur a mercatoribus sunt maiores; ubi vero revenduntur sunt minores. Similiter autem iura legalia non naturalia sed humana, id est humanitus posita, non sunt eadem ubique, quia nec urbanitas nec modus vivendi homini sunt ubique eadem.

13.

In hoc autem apparet differentia utriusque iuris, quoniam ius naturale est id ubique, quamvis non semper, sicut praeeminentis dextrae super sinistram; ius vero legale non est idem ubique sicut nec mensurae. Item, quia variatio iuris naturalis contingit raro et in paucioribus, sicut raro contingit quod aliqui sint ambidextri. Variatio vero et diversitas iuris legalis est quasi semper, sicut diversitas et inaequalitas mensurarum.

14.

Ultimo (1135a3) autem concludit quod, quamvis secundum iura legalia varia et diversa diversae sint urbanitates et non eadem apud omnes, una tamen sola secundum naturam optima ubique esse potest. Quia non est possibile plures esse urbanitates optimas. Quare si ubique homines urbanizarent et politizarent, optime ubique necessario esset una urbanitas.

CHAPTER EIGHT: THE HEBREW COMMENTARIES

In this chapter, we will undertake an analysis of three distinct medieval Hebrew commentaries on the *Ethics*.[1] These commentaries exist solely in manuscript form, and we will provide their complete texts at the conclusion of this chapter. Each of these commentaries is founded upon one of three different Hebrew translations of Aristotle. Rabbi Joseph Ibn Kaspi's commentary is rooted in the Hebrew translation of Averroes by Rabbi Samuel son of Judah. Rabbi Joseph Ibn Shem-Tov's commentary is based on the translation by Rabbi Alguadez, while Rabbi Baruch ben Yaish's commentary (likely comprising notes from one of his students) draws from his own translation. Throughout the chapter, we will focus on highlighting the significant philosophical divergences between the commentators and the original text upon which their commentaries are based, as well as their deviations from the original Greek.

---

[1] We will also exclude the analysis of two anonymous commentaries on the *Ethics*, one of which is complete while the other is only partial, as well as the early modern commentary of Moses Almosnino.

Rabbi Joseph Ibn Kaspi

Rabbi Joseph Ibn Kaspi (1280-1345)[2] is one of the most prominent philosophers of the Jewish Averroist movement that flourished in Provence, Italy, and Spain in the fourteenth and fifteenth centuries. His commentary on ethics is part of his book *Trumat HaKessef* (The Donation of Silver), which interprets Plato's *Republic*[3] and Aristotle's ethics. The section dealing with the *Republic* was published by Sackson, but the section discussing ethics still exists only in manuscript form.

As evidenced in the text in appendix of this chapter, most of the passage reveals that Rabbi Kaspi predominantly reproduces or offers a condensed rephrasing of Averroes' explanations. Consequently, his stance largely coincides with that of Averroes. Nevertheless, a meticulous examination of the disparities exposes a substantial deviation that carries philosophical implications from Averroes' commentary.[4]

The most significant disparity concerning the theory of natural law pertains to Rabbi Kaspi's limitation of its

---

[2] Regarding the life, work, and philosophical positions of Rabbi Kaspi, the following sources have been examined: Cohen 2015; Mesch 1975; Herring 1982; Sirat 1983, pp. 133-141; Aslanov 2002; Kasher 2006; Ben-Shalom 2010; Sackson 2016, pp. 28-71. Regarding his interpretation of the Torah, I have consulted Rak 2007, pp. 1-129.

[3] Furthermore, as will be mentioned later regarding the translation of the *Ethics*, Rabbi Kaspi closely follows the commentary of Averroes.

[4] Numerous philosophical divergences can be found within *Trumat HaKessef* (The Donation of Silver), as evidenced by Sackson's analysis of the sections pertaining to the *Republic*.

scope to "a few universal laws" (קצת הנימוסים שהם אחדים לכל). According to Rabbi Kaspi, natural laws are scarce, and their observance is not only universally necessary (as advocated by Averroes) but also observed in practice in every society. Averroes' position can be interpreted as endorsing the possibility of a society that disregards any aspect of natural law – such a society would not be deemed moral, yet the violation of a specific injunction does not automatically negate its connection to natural law.[5] Conversely, according to Rabbi Kaspi's interpretation, natural law is indeed embraced by all extant societies.[6] This standpoint diminishes the concept of natural law, prompting Rabbi Kaspi to assert that it consists merely of "a few laws", a notion absent in Averroes' commentary or the original Greek source of the chapter.

---

[5] Although the statement "However, they naturally will not change, for they are imperative everywhere and at all times, like fire, whose power is the same in every place" (ואולם אשר הם בטבע הנה לא יתחלפו אחר שהיה כחם אחד בכל מקום וזמן כמו האש אשר כוחה אחד בכל מקום) in Averroes's words does suggest that a society violating natural law is implausible (due to the association between the universality of natural law and its immutability), it is important to note that this sentence is part of the argument put forth by "some individuals" (קצת האנשים). Therefore, it is unnecessary to interpret it as representative of Aristotle's stance (in Averroes' commentary). According to this interpretation, those individuals argue that natural law must indeed be present in every society, but it does not necessarily align with Aristotle's position. Nevertheless, Rabbi Kaspi's words elucidate the connection between natural law and its recognition by all societies worldwide more clearly than Averroes' statements.

[6] These matters are in tension with the statements of R. Kaspi in other works. On this subject, see Sadik 2017.

Rabbi Joseph Ibn Shem-Tov

Rabbi Joseph Ibn Shem-Tov, a prominent intellectual from Castile who died in 1480, exhibited a conservative mindset coupled with a remarkable command of philosophy.[7] His extensive commentary on the *Ethics* gained significant recognition, with eighteen attributed manuscripts. As evidenced by Chaim Neria's research, Rabbi Joseph based his interpretations on the translation by Rabbi Alguadez, which is also found in several of his manuscripts. Furthermore, he exhibits familiarity with Averroes's commentary, acquired through the Hebrew translation by Rabbi Samuel ben Judah. It appears that Rabbi Joseph presents a complex yet consistent approach reflecting Aristotle's intention in his commentary on chapter V.7.

I.

In the opening of the initial paragraph, Rabbi Joseph demonstrates a strong connection to his primary source, Rabbi Alguadez. However, it becomes evident that Rabbi Joseph is also well-versed in Averroes' commentary, as indicated by his use of the terms דתי (derived from Rabbi

---

[7] For an examination of Rabbi Joseph Ibn Shem-Tov's philosophy, refer to the research of Ragev 1993, as well as the doctoral dissertation by Neria, which specifically explores his commentaries on ethics. Regarding his concept of happiness (primarily related to his commentaries on ethics), see also Tirosh-Samuelson 2003. Rothschild 2016 should be consulted for an introduction to the commentary. For the history of the family and their relationship to philosophical thought, refer to Guttman 1913. It should be noted that Porti 2017 argued that Shem Tov Ibn Shem-Tov II (in contrast to the first, the father of Joseph Ibn Shem-Tov) was a radical philosopher, contrary to Guttman's claim.

Alguadez's translation) and נימוסי (derived from Averroes' *Compendium*) to refer to conventional laws. Rabbi Joseph's main contribution to his analysis of the *Ethics* reflects his religious perspective rather than his interpretation of Aristotle. He confidently asserts that there are no inherent justifications for commandments prior to their enactment, such as the practice of marrying two sisters, which was not considered problematic before the introduction of the Torah's commandment and was only prohibited thereafter.

This example holds significant importance as it illuminates Rabbi Joseph's broader understanding of conventional commandments that surpasses the requirements outlined in the passage. Although Jacob did marry two sisters, which prompted Rabbi Joseph to introduce this example, one could have assumed that only Moses understood the rationale behind this commandment, which existed even before its formal promulgation (a viewpoint supported by Maimonides). Within this section, Rabbi Joseph embraces Aristotle's dichotomy: the natural realm remains unchanging, while the conventional sphere is contingent upon contextual factors and the decisions of authoritative figures (whether political or religious, as Rabbi Joseph does not differentiate between them in his discourse, mentioning them parenthetically).

In the concluding part of the initial paragraph, Rabbi Joseph embraces Averroes' (and Thomas's) addition and posits the existence of natural principles within conventional laws. The fundamental divergence between Rabbi Joseph and Averroes resides in the illustrative instances they employ to elucidate conventional laws, namely, murder, adultery, and theft. These examples serve as the foundational pillars of any natural legal framework. Consequently, Rabbi Joseph effectively establishes that even within the realm of natural laws, their specific applications are conventional and subject to relativity. This standpoint stands in contrast to Averroes, who espoused the contrary notion that even conventional laws are underpinned by natural principles. Thus, the inaugural paragraph of Rabbi Joseph's commentary culminates with the understanding that he discerns between religious and conventional commandments devoid of inherent natural rationales, and natural commandments that possess a general nature while their specifics are contingent on convention.

II.

At the outset of the second paragraph, Rabbi Joseph makes no substantial contributions. He simply establishes a connection between Aristotle's remarks on the mutability of conventions and the teachings of the Sages of the Mishna (first part of the oral law) concerning the authority of one court to nullify a decree issued by another court. In the latter portion of the paragraph, Rabbi Joseph elucidates the divine matters, referred to as הדברים האלוהים, which remain unchanging and pertain to metaphysical truths associated with God and distinct intellects. Conversely, he asserts that even moral and natural matters experience some degree of change, a concept he expounds upon further in the subsequent paragraph. Thus, Rabbi Joseph effectively comprehends the second interpretation mentioned in Rabbi Alguadez's text: while metaphysics remains immutable, matters of morality undergo changes in all domains, including the natural realm. There exists no absolute and unchanging natural morality that universally applies across all times, places, and circumstances.

In the third paragraph, Rabbi Joseph presents an intriguing novelty in his interpretation of the parable of the left hand and the right hand, influenced by Thomas Aquinas's commentary.[8] According to his understanding, this parable signifies that all moral and natural matters (in contrast to metaphysics) are essentially probabilistic. For instance, even natural laws, such as the restitution of a deposit, contain exceptions.[9] One could further argue, following Rabbi Joseph's approach, that there might be circumstances in which murder is justified, for example by the hypothetical scenario of killing Adolf Hitler in 1934, because of exceptions within every moral rule. This interpretation holds particular significance as Rabbi Joseph reconciles the dual implications of Aristotle's words, as well as those of Rabbi Alguadez. From his perspective, the change indicated by Aristotle in natural moral laws pertains to their non-absoluteness and presence of exceptions, distinguishing them from the laws of nature and metaphysics.[10]

---

[8] Rabbi Joseph draws upon Thomas Aquinas's commentary, although his conclusions diverge significantly. Aquinas's interpretation espouses a clear understanding of a cohesive natural law and morality, which is also discernible in the commentary of this chapter. This is especially conspicuous in his elucidation of the passage addressing laws, wherein he emphasizes that only one law is inherently natural and universally applicable.

[9] This interpretation resembles the positions of Strauss 1999 and Yack 1990.

[10] For a contemporary perspective on this matter, see Corbett 2009. According to Corbett, Aristotle's view suggests that there is no law that possesses absolute correctness. Consequently, the living

III.

Furthermore, in the subsequent passage, Rabbi Joseph elucidates the precise differentiation: natural law encompasses principles that possess universal applicability across all locations and societies (such as the prohibitions against murder and theft). Conversely, conventional laws are specific to particular societies (such as the prohibition of marrying one's sister or specific regulations pertaining to sacrificial rituals). The defining characteristic of natural laws lies in their acceptance by all societies, rather than their absolute correctness in every circumstance. Within any given society, there may exist extreme situations in which the act of murder is justifiable, or the non-restitution of a deposit is deemed acceptable. It is also noteworthy that within Rabbi Joseph's discourse, there is a concurrence that exceptional circumstances may arise in which religious law is temporarily suspended for individuals who are generally bound by it (as exemplified by Elijah's offering of sacrifices on Mount Carmel).[11]

At the conclusion of the text, Rabbi Joseph eliminates the term "alone" (לבד), thereby altering the interpretation of the passage and rendering the textsupport for relativism

---

law of the king, which has the power to modify laws in specific circumstances, holds a position of superiority over written law. This interpretation has significantly influenced the viewpoints of numerous Jewish philosophers, including Maimonides and Rabbi Nissim Gerondi, regarding the king's ability to repeal laws. For a more comprehensive exploration of this subject, see Loberbaum 2002.

[11] This subject pertains to the inquiry on equity and its correlation with divine law. Within the realm of Hebrew commentary on the *Nicomachean Ethics*, see Sadik 2023.

highly implausible. In contrast, the possibility of a relativistic interpretation is evident in the writings of Rabbi Alguadez.

Therefore, we can conclude that in his interpretation, Rabbi Joseph puts forth a nuanced and coherent position. He distinguishes between natural laws and conventional (or religious) laws. Conventional laws exhibit variations in their entirety and specifics across different societies. On the other hand, natural laws are universal in their existence across all societies as a whole, while their specifics are subject to variation, rendering them fundamentally conventional. Furthermore, even the principles of natural law (as well as the conventional laws of a particular society) can be suspended in extreme circumstances. As a result, they do not possess the inherent universality of physical laws of nature (such as a burning fire) or of metaphysical conclusions.

Rabbi Baruch Ibn Yaish

In his commentary, Rabbi Baruch presents a cohesive perspective that regards all laws as mutable yet still specific manifestations of immutable natural principles. According to his interpretation, there exists no realm of religious or conventional laws that does not ultimately represent particular instances of natural laws.[12]

---

[12] Hence, one can discern both the direct and indirect impact of Averroes, and notably, the profound influence stemming from Thomas Aquinas's interpretation. However, a clear distinction arises between these two philosophers and Rabbi Baruch. While Thomas advocates for an absolute conception of natural morality, Rabbi Baruch posits that all specific applications are relative. Thus, Rabbi Baruch's stance diverges even from that of Averroes,

I.

In the opening paragraph of his commentary, Rabbi Baruch employs the term דתי (religious) in a manner consistent with his translation, to characterize conventional laws that diverge from the natural realm. Subsequently, he introduces the terms הנחי (directive) and הסכמי (consensual). At the outset of the paragraph, no notable disparities arise between his viewpoint and that of his sources. Nevertheless, he proceeds to define natural laws as enduring and ubiquitous, while depicting the religious or conventional (resulting from consensus), as displaying variability across nations and regions (where climate serves as a determinant factor).

The primary shift in the initial paragraph occurs subsequently, as Rabbi Baruch (under the influence of Thomas Aquinas) elucidates that religious (or conventional) laws derive from natural laws in two distinct ways. Certain conventional laws inherently emanate from natural laws, such as the redemption of captives, which constitutes a religious (or conventional) law that unavoidably arises from the inherent freedom of human beings. Conversely, there exist conventional laws that derive from natural laws as specific manifestations of a general principle—these represent distinct conventional laws (termed religious laws). Illustrative examples of such laws encompass the precise valuation of captive

---

who espouses the existence of an immutable category of natural laws.

redemption or specific regulations pertaining to sacrificial rituals.[13]

According to Rabbi Baruch, three categories of laws can be delineated: 1. natural laws (such as human freedom and the obligation to serve God), 2. religious laws (or conventional laws) that possess an intrinsic natural essence (including redemption of captives and the necessity for sacrifices), and 3. religious laws that constitute specific instances derived from natural laws (comprising the mechanism of captive redemption and the detailed particulars of sacrificial rituals).[14]

II.

In the second paragraph, the significant additions revolve around Rabbi Baruch's rejection of the blanket denieal of the existence of universal laws. Initially, Rabbi Baruch argues that natural phenomena appear to vary from our perspective, although in reality they do not vary (וזה כי הם אינם משתנים – אבל אצלנו יהיה כבר דבר מה טבעי משתנה [and this is because they do not vary - but for us, something natural will be something that varies]). The implication of his statements becomes clearer in the third paragraph. Like Rabbi Joseph, Rabbi Baruch is also influenced by Thomas Aquinas and contends that natural phenomena

[13] Rabbi Baruch posits that the act of offering sacrifices constitutes a natural law emanating from a broader natural law that imposes upon humans the obligation to worship their Creator. This particular example does not originate from the teachings of Thomas Aquinas or Maimonides, both of whom maintain significantly different perspectives on the subject of sacrifices.

[14] This interpretation of Aristotle aligns more closely with the contemporary perspective of Burns 2011, pp. 48-58.

can maintain their validity despite being open to suspension in exceptional circumstances. Additionally, Rabbi Baruch reaffirms Aristotle's position that there are both natural laws and conventional laws.

III.

In the third paragraph, similar to Rabbi Joseph (and under the influence of Thomas Aquinas), Rabbi Baruch employs the metaphor of hands to elucidate the capacity for natural laws to undergo changes in human beings while retaining their inherent nature. According to the order of nature, the right hand is deemed stronger, despite exceptions — such as individuals who possess equal proficiency with both hands. It is noteworthy that Rabbi Baruch diverges from Rabbi Joseph (and approaches Aquinas) by attributing superiority to the general natural state. The exceptional state, wherein an individual employs both hands equally, is regarded as less desirable than the natural state where right-handedness prevails. This perspective deviates from Aristotle's original intent in the analogy and may even present a contradiction. Aristotle posits that conventional laws enhance the existing natural state, whereas Rabbi Baruch maintains that the natural state is always preferable. In generalizing this notion, Rabbi Baruch can argue that returning a deposit is always morally superior to not returning it. This opinion closely aligns with Aquinas's stance on natural morality. Different moral laws are tailored to suit various nations and states. However, on the contrary, there exists an ideal state where the most impeccable natural law finds its applicability. Consequently, Rabbi Baruch contends that there is an absolute natural morality that includes different laws, but its suitability extends solely to one ideal society rather than every nation. In other scenarios, laws must be adjusted according to necessity, notwithstanding the fact that these requirements stem from underlying deficiencies or vices that impede an individual's attainment of absolute moral perfection.

We observe this stance in the example provided by Rabbi Baruch in the subsequent passage:[15] there is a law that aligns with the disposition of individuals residing in the central regions of the globe (near the equatorial axis)—who are inherently more inclined towards engaging in illicit sexual relations (based on the theory of climates espoused by Rabbi Baruch). This law, which exhibits greater stringency in exposing illicit relations, is considered optimal for such promiscuous individuals. However, upon reflection, it would have been more desirable for the temperament of these individuals to be colder, resulting in reduced promiscuity. An ideal scenario necessitates a different law that is incongruous with the negative state of these inherently promiscuous individuals.[16]

---

[15] This analogy is not found in the writings of Thomas Aquinas.

[16] Surrounding the evolution of legal principles, Rabbi Baruch's standpoint diverges from that of Burns 2011. Burns posits that natural laws remain constant, while only their expressions vary across diverse societies, pp. 62-58. In this context, Rabbi Baruch's perspective aligns more closely with the views presented by Duke 2020 and Destree 2000. According to Duke and Destree, Aristotle regards natural law as a standard according to which one can discern the varying degrees of perfection among established conventional laws. Rabbi Baruch departs from this position by maintaining that conventional law solely addresses specific instances. However, according to his view, different

Rabbi Baruch and Rabbi Joseph adopt divergent approaches in their interpretations of Thomas Aquinas's discourse concerning the predominance of moral natural laws and their exceptions. Rabbi Joseph maintains that natural laws have universal applicability across societies but exhibit unique deviations within each specific society. This view delineates a separate realm for natural laws alongside a distinct domain for conventional or religious laws, which, as observed, both undergo infrequent modifications under extreme circumstances. Conversely, Rabbi Baruch's interpretation posits that these deviations correspond to societies existing in an imperfect state, thereby necessitating the establishment of distinctive moral codes that diverge from the idealized concept of natural morality. Rabbi Baruch's stance aligns more closely with Thomas Aquinas original position, while Rabbi Joseph's perspective bears greater resemblance to the illustrative examples put forth by Aristotle, such as the redemption of captives.

The degree to which Rabbi Baruch's stance aligns with his observations made at the beginning of the chapter regarding the relationship between conventional (or religious) laws and natural laws is not entirely discernible from his commentary. While he does reiterate the notion that conventional laws are specific manifestations of natural laws in the concluding paragraph, the precise alignment remains ambiguous. An important question arises: does a comprehensive conventional law exist that encompasses all the diverse particulars within it, or are gradations of conventional laws exist, which can be assessed in accordance with the overarching principles of human nature.

there highly distinct laws in which the particulars lack inherent significance until they are determined (such as specific laws pertaining to sacrifices)? The latter possibility seems to be the correct one, seeing as Rabbi Baruch clearly asserts that there is a limitation to natural morality. In matters involving intricate detail, they are entirely conventional or ritualistic, devoid of any inherent natural meaning.

Rabbi Baruch's commentary can be succinctly characterized as endorsing the concept of natural morality and the resultant natural law. While there exist variations in the understanding of optimal laws and moral norms across different societies, these divergences stem from unfavorable circumstances that hinder individuals residing in imperfect societies from attaining a state in which natural law and morality are within their grasp. In an ideal scenario, religious and conventional laws would partly emanate from society's ideal natural state, albeit to a limited extent, such as in the case of sacrificial practices involving goats or sheep. Among the Hebrew commentators, Rabbi Baruch emerges as the most articulate advocate of the notion of a universal natural law and morality.

Summary

This chapter explores three distinct Hebrew commentaries on the *Ethics* that demonstrate a greater coherence in Aristotle's views compared to the original Greek or the various translations upon which they are based. Rabbi Kaspi, in particular, works with Averroes' *Compendium*, which not only enhances the consistency of Aristotle's own perspective but also establishes a clear division between natural law that remains unchanging and conventional law that encompasses both natural categories and relativistic specific applications. Rabbi Kaspi maintains the stance of Averroes, while constraining natural laws to those universally accepted within any given society.

Contrary to this position, according to Rabbi Joseph Ibn Shem-Tov, conventional (or religious) laws exhibit variations in both their specific content and nature, while natural laws maintain a consistent nature but exhibit variations in their specific manifestations according to societal context. Another notable contribution by Rabbi Joseph Ibn Shem-Tov is the assertion that all laws, encompassing both natural and conventional principles within their respective societies, possess the potential to undergo modifications in extraordinary or exceptional circumstances. Consequently, Rabbi Joseph challenges the concept of a universal natural law, contending that ethical principles can necessitate the suspension of any law in particular situations.

In contrast to this stance, Rabbi Baruch interprets Aristotle as an ardent proponent of moral natural law. According to Rabbi Baruch, conventional laws represent relatively peripheral aspects of the comprehensive and uniform natural law present across all domains. Although certain societies may deviate from adherence to natural laws (and it may even be better for them to do so due to their adverse conditions for upholding such lofty moral standards), such societies are considered inferior to those that uphold the precepts of natural law.

The different Jewish commentators offer varying opinions regarding the definition of natural law and the extent to which it plays a central role. Rabbi Kaspi argues for the existence of only a few natural laws, while Rabbi

Baruch contends that most laws fall under the domain of natural law. Rabbi Joseph Ibn Shem-Tov holds a moderate stance on this subject.

A common thread among these commentaries is the division between categories and specific laws. Although this division does not appear in Aristotle's original text, it can be inferred from his examples and is influenced by the works of Averroes and Thomas Aquinas (who himself drew inspiration from Averroes). Interestingly, this distinction is not affirmed by the known Arabic translation or the Byzantine commentators, indicating that Aristotle's text can be comprehended without it.

Texts of the Hebrew Commentaries.

Trumat HaKessef (The Donation of Silver)[17]

The vast majority of the excerpts are a replication of the elucidations provided by Averroes. Those passages which have been added by Rabbi Kaspi have been placed in bold type: a comparative analysis with the preceding explanation reveals that he also omitted certain sections of the excerpts.

I.

אמר השווי[18] קצתו טבעיי נימוסי וקצתו נימוסי לבד ר"ל הנחי. ואולם השווי הטבעי הנה הוא **ה**שווי אשר כוחו אחד בכל מקום ובכל זמן **ובכל אומה** ולא תפול בו תמורה **וזה העניין נמצא בקצת הנימוסים שהם אחדים לכל**. ואולם הנימוסי אשר איננו טבעי הנה הוא אם בסוג הוא כאלו הוא טבעי **כי הסוג אין בו תמורה ואולם** בשעירת הזבחים והקרבנות המונחות בדתות והתורות.

II.

וקצת האנשים יסברו שכל השווים הנימוסיים ההנחיים **אשר אינם טבעיים** יפול בם תמורה ושינוי כפי שיראה מניח ממניחי הנימוסים להיות **החילוף ביניהם מצד מה, שהם רואים** היותר נאות כפי הזמן והמקום. ואולם אשר הם בטבע הנה לא יתחלפו אחר שיהיה כחם אחד בכל מקום וזמן כמו האש אשר

---

[17] Taken from the manuscript, Vienna, Österreichische Nationalbibliothek, cod. Hebr. 27; Microfilm Catologue of the Israel National Library F 1305 : 24 r.

[18] Rabbi Joseph ibn Kaspi removed the term, מדיני (political), from the text.

HEBREW COMMENTARIES

כוחה אחד בכל מקום, רצוני שהיא תתנועע למעלה באי זו פאה הונחה מן העולם ובאי זו עת הונחה.

III.

הנה יהיו הדברים השווים כפי זה מהם פועלים לשווי מפני הטבע ומהם פועלים מפני המנהג לא מפני טביעתם באיכותם אבל מפני ההנחה והעשיה להם. וכמו שהיד הימנית היא ימנית בטבע והשמאלית **שמאלית בטבע אבל השמאלית תשוב** ימנית בהרגל כן העניין בשווים הטבעיים והרגליים. **ואלו ההרגליים יתחלפו כפי אומה ואומה וכפי חילוף השיעור בם כמו שמדות החיטה והיין וזולת זה ממה שיפלו בם השיעורים אינם אחדים לכל האומות.**[19]

---

[19] Rabbi Kaspi provides a very concise paraphrase of Ibn Rushd's commentary.

The commentary of Joseph Ibn Shem-Tov[20]

In what follows, I have indicated citations from Rabbi Alguadez's translation through the use of bold type.[21]

I.

ואחר שביאר מציאות הצדק המדיני ואמתתו, נעתק לבאר הבדליו. ואמר **הצדק המדיני ממנו טבעי וממנו דתי**, ירצה היושר המדיני נחלק לשני חלקים ממנו טבעי וממנו נימוסי. עוד ביאר אותם ואמר **הטבעי אשר הוא בכל מקום**[22] **יש לו כוח שווה ואינו תלוי בראות או לא**. ירצה הצדק הטבעי הוא אשר הוא שוה בכל מקום ובכל זמן וזה הכח הוא שוה שיגע אל הטוב ולהסיר מהרע. סור מרע ועשה טוב. והוא לפי המעלה בהחלט לא יקבל תמורה,[23] שאינו תלוי לפי ראות עיני הדיין[24]

---

[20] I drew upon manuscript Paris 996 from Kaufmann 14681 (number 1 in Neria's list), pp. 185a-186b. I also compared, when necessary, with the manuscript Moscow Günzburg 542 from Kaufmann 17381 (number 13 in Neria's list) as presented by Neria in his doctoral dissertation, pp. 89a-89b, and with the manuscript document Paris 997 from Kaufmann 14682, pp. 143b-145a. It is highly plausible that the two latter handwritten documents originate from the same branch copied from the first one since all three exhibit the exact absence of a complete line.

[21] There are differences between the words of Aristotle in Rabbi Alguadez's translation and their quotations in Rabbi Joseph's writings. In these instances, I have preserved the wording as it appears in the manuscript Paris 996 of Rabbi Joseph's commentary.

[22] Here, there is a missing line in the Moscow manuscript. The fact that the same line is precisely missing suggests that this manuscript was copied from the Paris manuscript 996, pp. 143b-145a.

[23] Here, there is also a short missing section in Paris 997.

HEBREW COMMENTARIES

שהניחוהו. והרציחה בהחלט הוא רע איננו תלוי בראות או לא, ונקרא טבעי להיות הטבע אחד לכל הדברים ובכל מקום וזמן. עוד ביאר היושר הנימוסי. ואמר **הדתי אמנם הוא אשר בראשונה לא היה בו חילוק שיהיה כן או בענין אחר אבל אחר שהושם יש בו חילוק**. ירצה ואולם הצדק הדתי הנה הוא אשר קודם שהונח וסודר מאנשי הדת לא היה הפרש שיהיה כן או בענין אחר אבל אחר שהושם יש בו חילוק כמו הלקיחה לשתי אחיות לנשים שבראשונה, קודם שהונח בתורה, אין חילוק בין שיקח אותם אם לא ולא, היה נקרא צדיק בהרחיקו מהן, ולא בלתי שווה בקחתו אותן אחר שהושם בדת, יש בו חלוקה גדול בין שיקח שתי אלו לנשים או לא שאם יקח אותם הוא בלתי שוה שעבר על דת. הנה הצדק הנימוסי אשר איננו טבעי הוא מעולה אצל המניח הדת ואולם הטבעי הוא מעולה במוחלט. כי קודם מתן תורה שהיו אנשי סדום רעים וחוטאים השיג אותם העונש הנפלא לעובר על הצדק ולזה ספר רוע ענינם אצל האורחים כמו שעשו אנשי הגבעה וכולם עבדו היושר הטבעי מלבד היושר הנימוסי האלוהי. וזהו אמרו **כמו שיהיה פדיון העבד שער ידוע ולזבוח עז ולא צאן**, בזה ירצה שיהיה פדיון העבד שיעור ידוע ושיזבחו עז ולא ב רחלות הנה אלה המשפטים הם נימוסיים מונחים לא טבעיים שקודם שיצווה בתורה אין רע לעבור עליהם ואולם אחר הנחתם הוא רשע ופשע. בחלוף הטבעי שקודם מתן תורה ואחר מתן תורה הלא הוא יושר ועבור עליו ענין מגונה מאוד. עוד אמר **וגם כן הדת אשר ישימו למיוחדים כמו לזבוח לבשאירה**. ירצה וגם כן היושר הנימוסי תסודר לאיזה חלקי ופרטי כמו שקרה במדינה שהסכימו לזבוח לאשה אחת חסידה תועלת גדולה מהמדינה. הנה הנימוסי הוא בצד מה טבעי והוא בכללות, כמו הרחקת החמס והגזילה והניאוף, וזולתם שהוא נימוסי יוצא מן הטבעי.

---

[24] Rabbi Joseph explains the word ראות as symbolizing the personal opinion of the judge (ראות עיניו).

182 NATURAL LAW

ואולם שעירתם שיהיה עונש הגנב חמש בקר תחת השור וארבעה צאן תחת השה, ושאר השערות אינו טבעי אבל הוא מתחלף כפי אומה ומלכות מלכות גם מדינה ומדינה.

II.

עוד אמר והדינים יראה לקצת כי כולם הם כמו שאינם טבעים כי אשר הוא טבעי לא יסור ובכל מקום יהיה לו הכוח ההוא כמו האש אשר היא שורפת הנה ופרס אמנם הצדקות תראה שהם נעות. ירצה וכבר חשבו אנשים שהשווים כלם הנימוסיים הם הנחיים ואינם טבעיים כלל וזו סברה סקרטס[25] ואולם חשב זה, בעבור שאשר בטבע לא ישתנה ולא יתנועע אבל בכל מקום כחו הוא אחד כמו כח האש שהוא טבעי על השריפות שתשרוף ביון ובפרס. ואמנם הדינים והמשפטים יראה שהם יסורו בסור הסיבה שמה שהיה מהם טוב בזמן מה יראה שהוא רע בזמן אחר, וכן בא ב״ד פלוני והתיר אשר אסרו ב״ד פלוני אם יהיה גדול ממנו בחכמה ובמנין. ואם יהיה השווי ההוא טבעי לא יהיה משתוה עוד נעתק לבטל זאת הסברא. ואמר **אמנם יראה שזה אינו כן אבל הוא כי אע״פ שהדברים האלוהים הם קיימים וחזקים אינם כן הדברים אשר אצלנו.** ירצה אמנם יראה שזאת הסברא בטלה ואינו כן, אבל הוא כי אע״פ שהדברים הטבעיים בלתי משתנים יצדק זה בקצתם ולא בכולם כמו הדברים האלוהיים שהם האלוה והשכלים הנבדלים כי המלאכים כשם שהם חזקים וקיימים לא ישיגם הפסד ושינוי

---

[25] Rabbi Joseph presented the view that this is the opinion of Socrates from the words of Thomas Aquinas, who attributes this view explicitly to Aristippus Socraticus. This involves a mistaken substitution between Socrates and his student, Aristippus of Cyrene, who held very different positions. It is possible that the source of this mistake lies in the anonymous Hebrew commentary, which is a kind of paraphrase of Thomas's interpretation.

HEBREW COMMENTARIES

ותמורה, אבל אינם כן הדברים הטבעיים אשר אצלנו כי אנחנו
עם היותנו טבעיים כבר אפשר שישתנו ויתנועעו. ואמרו כי היה
שם דבר טבעי רע גמור בהצטרף אלינו כמו שיהיה שם ג״כ טוב
מוחלט טבעי בהצטרף אלינו. אבל יהיה שם בשווי דבר טבעי
ודבר שאינו טבעי אבל נימוסי.

III.

ועוד נעתק להעיר ספק על זה. ואמר **ועל כל אמנם טבע דברים
אשר יקרה היותם והם מתחלפים. איך נדע איזה הם בטבע
ואיזה לא כי אם בתשומת דתית.** ירצה ועל כן ישאר ספק
ומבוכה, והיא שטבע הדברים אשר יקרה היותם שוים בטבע
והם ג״כ מתחלפים ומשתנים כמו שישתנו הנימוסים ואשר הם
בהנחה א״כ איך נדע במה נכיר מה שהם שוים בטבע ואשר
אינם בטבע כי אם בתשומה תורנית אחר ששניהם משתנים
ומתנועעים. והוא אמרו **אם שניהם נעים גלוי ובשאר הדברים
הטבעיים – כן צריך אל ביאור.** ירצה ואחר שהשוויים ההנחיים
נעים ונדים ובשאר הדברים הטבעיים השוים ג״כ נעים ונדים
ומתחלפים הנה צריך אל ביאור במה נכיר אלה מאלה? עוד
נעתק אל התשובה ואמר: **הימין בטבע הוא חזק ואם יקרה
שיהיה אדם ימיני בשני צדדיו.** ירצה הדברים הטבעיים כבר
יקרה היותם על הרוב ואם ישתנו הוא על המעט כמו הימין
שהוא בטבעי יותר חזק מהשמאל אם שכבר יקרה על המיעוט
שאדם יהיה ימיני בשני צדדיו עד שלא יהיה הימין ממנו יותר
חזק מהשמאל אם שכבר יקרה[26] לשוה הטבעי שהוא שוה ברוב
וישתנה על המיעוט. כמו השבת הפיקדון והשבת גמול והשבת
אבדה ודומיהם שהם שוים בטבע ועל הרוב ואם כבר אפשר
שישתנו באישים מה ובעניינים מה אבל הוא על המעט[27] ולכן
יסכימו עליהם כל האומות וכן הדעות הטבעיות. עוד ביאר עניין

---

[26] These three words follow the reading provided by Paris 997.

[27] Here there is a clear influence from the commentary of Thomas Aquinas.

השוים הנימוסים. ואמר **אמנם אשר הם כפי התשומה הם דברים צדיקים מועילים. הם דומים למדות כי אינם בכל מקום מדות היין והחטה שוות, אבל במקום שהם נקנים הם גדולות, אמנם במקום שהם נמכרים הם קטנות.** ירצה ואולם אשר יהיה שוה בהנחה ובהסכמה תורנית הם דברים שום מועילים במקומות מיוחדים ובזמנים מיוחדים, לא בכל המקומות כמו הטבעיים. אבל הם דומים למדות היין והחטה גדולות במקום אשר ימצאו שם יין וחטה בשפע והם קטנות במקומות אשר נמכרו שם, למעוט המצאם שם. הנה כל אחד מאלו המדות שוה במקומו ואינם אחדות בכל המקומות כן הוא השוי הנימוסי. כי המועיל לזאת המדינה וליושביה במקומו אינו מועיל ליתר המדינות ועל כן היה בכאן נימוס מיוחד ושם נימוס מיוחד. והוא אמרו: **כן הם הדברים בלתי טבעיים. אבל הדברים האנושיים יש כי הם אינם שווים בכל מקום כמו שישוב המדינות אינו שוה.** עוד אמר: **אבל אחד לבד הוא בכל מקום כפי הטבע נבחר.** ירצה אבל הצדק הטבעי הוא אחד נבחר בכל מקום על הרוב. ואמר **אמנם הצדקות והדברים אשר בדת כל אחד מהם הוא כמו הכללים שם הפרטים כי הדברים הנפעלים הם רבים אבל בכל אחד מאלה יש אחד הוא אחד כולל.** ירצה הדברים השוים והדברים אשר בנימוס הנה כל אחד מהם הוא כמו הכולל אל החלקים הנכנס תחתיו, כי הדברים הנפעלים הם רבים מתחלפים שעם שיש לכולם סדר אחד כולל כולם כבר יבוא זמן שראוי להחליפו כמו שאסרה התורה הבמות אחר בנין בית המקדש ובא אליהו לעשות קורבן בהר הכרמל להכרח, וגם הכל יודו שראוי להחזיר הפיקדון, אבל אם הפקיד זה חרב ביד זה וירצה לקחתו להרוג רעהו בסתר או בגלוי אין ראוי להשיבו אליו. הנה זהו אופן הסכמת היושר הטבעי והנימוסי ושינויים והבדלם ואופן הכרתם והם מאמרים בתכלית הגלוי.

Rabbi Baruch Ibn Yaish's commentary [28]

Here, bold type indicates the translation by R. Baruch.

I.

יאמר **כי היושר ממנו טבעי וממנו דתי ....** [29] כי היושר הוא פעל הצדק עשוהו הוא ב' מינים: הא' הוא טבעי, והב' הוא דתי. וביאר מה הוא המכוון באומרו שהיושר ממנו טבעי. ואמר **כי הטבעי הוא אשר בכל מקום יש לו כוח א' מבלתי חילוף**, וזהו ענין הדבר הטבעי. ובאמרו **לא א"כ יראה או לא**. ירצה כי אין הצדק הטבעי הוא אשר יראה לפי קצת שהוא כן או לא. ירצה **שהוא כן** אשר זהו ענין הצדק המונח בהסכמה. כי הוא צדק באקלים זולת אקלים ובמדינה זולת מדינה. ואמר **כי הדתי הוא אשר קודם הנחת הדת לא היה הפרש להיות כן או כענין אחר** כמו לבישת שעטנז אצלנו **אבל אמנם אחר נתינת הדת יש הפרש בניהם כמו להיות פדיון שבויים בשיעור ידוע ולזבוח עז וכו'** וראוי שתדע כי הצדק הדתי הנה הוא יוצא ומתחייב

---

[28] I employ, similar to Zonta, the manuscript Paris 1002 as a foundation and compare it to two other manuscripts when necessary. I made certain modifications based on the content of manuscript 1001. As we will observe, it is likely that manuscript 1003 was a reproduction of manuscript 1002, or that both originated from a common source. This chapter is explained there on pp. 147a-149a. Rabbi Baruch elucidates at the beginning of each section why Aristotle addresses this question here and what the relationship is between it and the preceding sections. Since Rabbi Baruch's commentary is extensive and there is no particular relevance to this explanation for our purposes, I have not included it here. I will also skip over some of his remarks that pertain to the context of the various chapters at the beginning of the commentary.

[29] At this point, Rabbi Baruch is dealing with the definition of righteousness. This is a topic unrelated to our subject.

מהצדק הטבעי אבל זה על ב' פנים: וזה כי המתחייב ויוצא מהצדק הטבעי על צד החיוב וההכרח הנה הוא ג"כ טבעית וזה על צד החיוב התולדה מהקדמות הכרחיות כי הנה התולדה ההיא היא הכרחית ולכן הצדק הדתי המתחייב מהטבעי על צד הכרח הנה היא טבעית.[30] המין הב' הוא מה שיוליד מהטבעית לא על צד ההכרח. משל הא' כאמרינו כי הצדק הטבעי הוא יהיה כל אדם מצד מה שהוא אדם חופשי ובן חורין כי האדם הוא כן בטבע. והנה יצא לנו מזה שאם יהיה אדם מה נמכר לצמיתות שהוא מן הראוי שיפדו אותו והנה זה הדין מן הצדק הדתי הוא מתחייב על צד הכרח מהצדק הטבעי והנה הוא גם כן טבעי. ומשל הב' כאמרך שראוי שיפדה האדם בכסף שלשים שקלים זהב או כמאה כסף. כי יתן איש כל הון ביתו הנה זהו בלתי מתחייב מהדתי (צריך להיות טבעי)[31] על צד החיוב וההכרח ולזה תקרה דתית והסכמית.[32] ולזה אמר **כי הדתי הוא אשר אחר נתינת הדת יש הפרש כמו לזבוח עז ולא שתי צאן.** וזה כי הזבח הוא דבר טבעי ראוי לכל אדם לעבוד את בוראו אשר לזה הזבחים אשר הדת צווה אותם הוא דבר טבעי. אמנם לזבוח עז ולא שתי צאן, הנה קודם נתינת הדת לא יהיה הפרש בין זה ובין זה. אם לא אחר נתינת הדת. וכן להיות פדיון שבויים בשיעור ידוע וזה כי פדיון שבויים[33] ואף אם הוא דתי הנה הוא מתחייב על צד החיוב מהטבעית הנה היותו בשיעור ידוע הוא

---

[30] This division, like a significant portion of the commentary on this section, originates from Thomas Aquinas's commentary on the same chapter.

[31] In the given context, it is most reasonable to have "natural", (טבעי) although in all manuscripts the reading is, "religious" (דתי).

[32] Both of the examples can also be found (with slight variations) in the commentary of Thomas Aquinas.

[33] Here, there is a missing line in the Paris manuscript 1003 (precisely the same line that could indicate that manuscript 1003 was copied manuscript 1002).

ענין הסכמיי. וכן לזבוח לבראשירה, והיא היתה אשה גדולה הסכימו בני מדינתה לעשות לה זבחים, הנה זה גם כן דתיי לא טבעי, וכן שאר הדינים מתחלפים בדתות.

II.

אמר **אמנם יראה לקצתם כלם הם כן וכו'**. הנה בזה יניח סברה קצת מן הפילוסופים, אשר היא מתחלפת ממאמר הפילוסופים הנה ויבטל אותה. ולזה יאמר כי אמנם יראה לקצת כי כל המשפטים הם כן כי כלם הם דתיים לא טבעיים, וזה כי אם היו טבעיים היו בלתי משתנים בהחלט, כי כן הוא כח הדבר הטבעי, כמו האש אשר הוא שורף הנה ובפראס, ואמנם כל המשפטים הם משתנים, אם כן הם בלתי טבעיים. אמר **אמנם זה אינו בזה דעת וכו'**. הנה יתחיל לבטל זאת הסברה מב' פנים: הא' ביטול הראיה אשר חייב מהדברים הטבעיים. והב' בביטול מה שעליו הראיה והוא אמרם כי כל המשפטים הם בלתי טבעיים. ואל הא' אמר שזה הענין ירצה על מה שאמרו שהדברים הטבעיים הם בלתי משתנים. ואמר כי בזה אין הענין כמו שיראו, שהם בלתי משתנים, כי אולי לא יהיה כן, וזה כי הם אינם משתנים – אבל אצלנו יהיה כבר דבר מה טבעי משתנה. אמ' **אמנם כי לא הכל אבל יש דבר טבעי וכו'**, הנה כי בזה ישאר כי אין הענין בדרוש המכוון הנה. ואמר[34] כי אצל המשפטים המדיניים הנה אף אם משתנים אשר בזה יראה שישתתפו לדברים אשר אצלנו הנה אמנם לא הכל הם טבעיים, כי לא כל המשפטים הם טבעיים אבל יש דבר מה טבעי ודבר מה בלתי טבעי.

III.

אמר **אמנם איך הוא אשר בטבע יוכל להיות משתנה וכו'**. ירצה בזה לספק ספק מה אשר בזה, ישלם ביאור מאמרו. והוא

---

[34] Here, we are dealing with a paraphrase and not a direct quotation, so I do not emphasize it.

מי הוא זה ואיזהו אשר עם היותו בטבע יוכל להיות משתנה. ואיך הוא אשר לא תשתנה כי אם בדת ובהנחה אחר ששניהם משתנים. ובמה ידע איפה מי הם המשפטים שיהיו טבעיים, ומי הם הבלתי טבעיים, כי יראה שאין ביניהם הפרש. אמר **הוא גלוי באחרים גם כן הביאור, יהיה א'** ירצה כי הנה זהו גלוי באחרים והם העניינים הטבעיים, רצונו: איך יהיו טבעיים אחר שהם משתנים. ומזה יהיה גלוי העניין במה שלפני כן, והוא איך יהיו קצת המשפטים טבעיים. ואם זה הם משתנים. כי הביאור בזה הוא א' וזה כי הימין לפי הטבע הוא היותר טוב, והיות האדם ימיני הוא היותר טוב, ואשר הוא על הרוב. אמנם כבר יקרה להיות משתנה על המעט והיות האדם ימיני משני צדדיו. ולא ימנע עם זה להיות הימין יותר טוב בטבע. וכן הענין הנה כי קצת המשפטים הם טבעיים ואפילו אם יקרה בהם השינוי. כמו מי שהפקיד כלי זין אצל זולתו כי כבר יקרה שאם ישיבם אליו יכה או יהרוג לזולתו, אשר לזה ראוי שלא ישיבם אליו. ואפילו אם השבת הפיקדון הוא משפט טבעי, וזה אמנם הוא על צד המקרה והזדמן. אמנם המשפטים אשר הם כפי ההנחה, הנה יקרה בהם מה שיקרו לדברים והמדות אשר בהם ישוערו וימדדו הדברים, וזה כי הם משתנים כפי שינוי המקומות. וכן גם כן המשפטים הבלתי טבעיים אינם אחדים בכל מקום, כפי התחלפות המקומות מזולתם כמו שגם לא יהיה ישוב המדינות א'. כאומרו כי המדינה המיושבת באמצע הישוב, הנה יושביה יהיו כפי מזגם יותר חמים מזולתם, אשר לזה יהיו פרוצים בעבירות יותר ולזה ראוי שיניחו שם הדין ועונשים למגלה עריות יותר מבזולת המקומות כי שם התקלה מצויה על הרוב. ועל זה ההקש בזולת. והנה יבא כי כח מהדברים המושגחים מהדת הם כמו הכוללים הפרטים כי הפרטים הנפעלים הם רבים וכל א' מתחלף לזולתו אשר לזה יקרה השינוי בהם כפי התחלפות המקומות. אמנם הכוללים לא יקרה בהם מהשינוי, אבל הם קיימים ומתחלפים והם אחדים בכל המקומות אשר לזה יקראו טבעיים.

CHAPTER NINE: CONCLUSION

In this scholarly investigation, we examine five distinct translations and eleven medieval commentaries pertaining to chapter V.7 of Aristotle's *Nicomachean Ethics*. These translations and commentaries originate from diverse linguistic, cultural, and religious contexts. The noteworthy aspect here is that philosophers of such varying backgrounds have chosen to articulate their philosophical views by providing commentaries on Aristotle's work, specifically addressing profound philosophical and religious questions. This phenomenon underscores the pivotal role of Aristotle and his *Ethics* within the multifarious contexts of the medieval Western world. Throughout the course of our analysis, we observe both internal cultural developments and points of convergence in interpretation among commentators and translators hailing from disparate backgrounds.

In the initial chapter, it becomes evident that Aristotle's text harbours internal tensions, which can give rise to diverse interpretations among readers and commentators. Certain passages within Aristotle's work invite a relativistic interpretation, while other sections within the same chapter unequivocally assert the existence of a natural law. In this conclusion, we shall summarize the principal philosophical interpretations, organized not by religious, linguistic, or chronological criteria, but rather by their philosophical tenor. We will begin with the most relativistic interpretations and conclude with those strongly endorsing an objective natural law.

Relativism

The two most relativistic interpretations are found in two specific translations: the Arabic rendition and the Hebrew translation attributed to R. Alguadez. Both translations introduce substantial alterations that either negate or circumscribe Aristotle's endorsement of an objective natural law, and in some instances, they incorporate supplementary elements that veer the text towards a relativistic standpoint. Notably, R. Alguadez introduces the notion of confining the objectivity of natural law exclusively to metaphysical beliefs—a viewpoint markedly distinct from the original text of Aristotle, which exclusively addresses political regulations. It is worth highlighting that the two Latin translations and Rabbi Baruch's Hebrew translation do not substantially amend Aristotle's original text (the first Latin translation makes only marginal adjustments favouring an objective natural law).

Rabbi Alguadez likely did not have access to the Arabic translation and relied instead on the first Latin translation, which emphasizes an objective natural law, as the foundational source for his own translation. Consequently, we can reasonably infer that these two translators espoused a relativistic interpretation rooted in their individual philosophical inclinations and their perceptions of Aristotle's prevailing philosophical stance.

While we do not discern any immediate and direct philosophical influence exerted by the Arabic translation, it is highly plausible that this rendition exerted an influence on medieval Muslim and Jewish relativist thinkers, such as Maimonides, and, in certain texts, Al-Farabi's. Rabbi Alguadez's translation notably wields a discernible philosophical impact on the commentary penned by Rabbi Joseph Ibn Shem-Tov.

The most conspicuously relativistic commentary is authored by Georgios Pachymeres, the third Byzantine commentator, who was certainly unacquainted with the Arabic translation and predates Rabbi Alguadez. The bulk of his commentary closely aligns with the two preceding Byzantine commentaries, yet he introduces a significant alteration towards the conclusion of his commentary. Here, he explicitly posits that the natural circumstances of each distinct country and context necessitate a distinct law that is intrinsic to it. Through this addition, Georgios espouses a relativistic viewpoint, seeing as in his interpretation, every place requires unique legal requisites. Therefore, each place and context possess its own distinctive conception of natural law, one that is not uniform across all contexts.

Non-relativists

In contrast to those commentators and translators who espouse a relativistic interpretation, all other commentators assert the existence of a form of natural law that remains consistent across all geographical *loci*, alongside conventional or legal laws that are subject to variation from one country to another, devoid of any inherent superiority.[1] The central inquiry for each of these commentators revolves around the definition and characteristics of both natural and conventional laws. It is evident that each commentator elucidates the precise

---

[1] The remaining translators do not introduce significant alterations to Aristotle's text and acknowledge its inherent ambiguity.

demarcation and interplay between these categories of law in their own distinct manner. Notably, as the scope of natural laws expand, philosophers tend to embrace an objective natural law perspective. Conversely, when conventional laws encompass not only specific details but also encompass broader categories of laws, such as the ideal form of governance, the philosopher leans towards a relativistic standpoint.

These commentaries can be categorized into two distinct trends:

1. The Averroist and Thomistic trend assert that conventional laws are essentially specifications of natural principles. It is also conceivable that certain natural laws may incorporate specific details. However, within this perspective, all conventional laws are regarded as elaborations or particularizations of natural principles.

2. Conversely, other philosophers, such as Albertus Magnus and the two first Byzantine commentators, either remain unaware of or do not concur with this interpretation. They contend that there exist two distinct realms of natural and conventional laws, encompassing both fundamental principles and specific details.

In the subsequent sections, we shall first provide a summary of the commentaries aligned with the second group of commentators, and subsequently, we will explore the commentaries influenced by the Averroist-Thomistic mode of interpretation.

Among these commentators, the one who adopts the most relativistic stance is our second Byzantine commentator, Michael of Ephesus. In his commentary, he restricts the domain of natural law to encompass only the most fundamental principles, such as the reverence for parents and deities. However, he explicitly maintains that fundamental laws like the prohibition of incest and the preferred form of governance belong to the realm of conventional laws, subject to alteration based on the unique circumstances prevailing in individual regions and countries.

The anonymous Byzantine commentator's perspective closely aligns with that of Michael. However, the absence of any mention of a similar limitation on natural law renders the former's commentary more inclined towards endorsing a broader conception of natural law. These two commentators also introduced a distinctive Byzantine notion that there are populations unable to adhere to the universal natural law due to adverse natural circumstances. This limitation, first introduced by the anonymous commentator, does not circumscribe the scope of natural law itself, but rather the feasibility of different human societies to adhere to these laws. According to their viewpoint, certain populations are not merely inferior due to their prevailing legal codes – codes that can be altered. Rather, they contend that some populations find themselves disadvantaged by their historical and cultural development (or innate disposition), rendering it wholly impracticable for them to observe the universal natural law that is the best to all humanity. In such cases, it is deemed more advisable for these populations to abide by a less exacting legal code that corresponds to their particular level of attainable perfection.

In this group of thinkers, Albertus Magnus emerges as a prominent advocate for an objective conception of natural law. He unequivocally asserts that there are individuals who adhere rigorously to the dictates of natural law. In his view, natural law is circumscribed by the constraints of both positive law, which varies within different societies, and divine law, which emanates from a singular source but remains non-natural due to its divine origin, transcending the bounds of rational human comprehension. Albertus Magnus not only references but also scrutinizes the position of Byzantine commentators who contended that certain populations lack the capacity to observe natural law. Contrary to this notion, Albertus Magnus posits that all human societies possess the inherent capability to adhere to natural law.

The second category of scholars tends to place more stringent limitations on conventional law due to the Averroes-Thomas interpretation, which finds unanimous acceptance among these thinkers. According to this interpretation, conventional law merely represents the specific application of natural principles. However, there are certain philosophers who have embraced this definition of natural law and consequently restricted the domain of natural laws to a very rudimentary set of principles, which, in fact, exhibit a more relativistic character compared to their counterparts from the former category of philosophers.

Among these thinkers, the one who adopts the most relativistic stance is the first Jewish commentator, Rabbi Joseph Ibn Kaspi. He offers commentary on the Hebrew translation of Averroes and adopts the definition of conventional laws as specific implementations of natural principles. Nevertheless, the notable aspect of his position lies in his limiting natural law to only those laws that are presently shared by all societies, thereby encompassing within the realm of natural laws only the most fundamental principles that have been universally prevalent throughout the history of human societies. To illustrate, under this definition, the prohibition of human sacrifice is excluded from the domain of natural law, as historical evidence indicates their practice among certain ancient peoples, such as the Phoenicians.

Rabbi Joseph Ibn Shem-Tov aligns closely with Rabbi Kaspi's perspective, asserting that even prohibitions against adultery and theft, though categorized as conventional law, maintain their natural principles while adapting to varying specific applications within different societies. Rabbi Joseph's viewpoint is notably influenced by the translation of Rabbi Alguadez, whose Hebrew text serves as the subject of his commentary. Rabbi Joseph posits that only metaphysics remains constant across all places and time, impervious to alteration under any circumstances.

Averroes, in his account, presents a clear dichotomy between two distinct categories of laws: natural laws, which exhibit uniformity across all places, encompassing both their foundational principles and specific applications; and conventional laws, characterized by their variable interpretations of natural principles. Notably, Averroes does not explicitly delineate the precise boundaries between these two realms, and his assertion that natural law remains consistent everywhere does not imply that these natural laws universally govern all countries but rather underscores the obligation for all nations to adhere to them.

Thomas Aquinas stands out as one of the foremost adherents of an objective conception of natural law. He embraces Averroes' view, asserting that conventional laws represent specific applications of natural principles, and delineates the domain of conventional law to encompass regulations pertaining solely to the animalistic aspects of human nature—a distinction absent in Averroes' framework. Notably, laws designed to cultivate the rational facet of human existence remain constant across all geographic and temporal contexts. In agreement with Byzantine commentators, Thomas also posits that deviations from natural law result from adverse circumstances within populations that practice erroneous laws. However, he diverges from the Byzantine tradition by contending that such circumstances do not preclude the possibility of rectifying the erroneous laws and adhering to the true and universally applicable natural law.[2] This stance places Thomas Aquinas in close proximity to his mentor, Albertus Magnus.

The viewpoints articulated by Radulphus and Geraldus closely parallel the perspective of Thomas Aquinas, with no significant departures observed concerning the issue of relativism among them. The primary distinction emerges between Thomas and Geraldus. The latter commentator permits an interpretation of Thomas's position, albeit with certain modifications, such as the omission of some of Thomas's unequivocal assertions (for instance, the assertion that all alterations in natural laws stem from

---

[2] The fact that Thomas maintains the stance that natural law need not be applied in exceptional circumstances, as exemplified by the example concerning the return of a sword in Plato's *Republic* I.331c, does not diminish the strength of his position regarding natural laws. Natural laws are those principles inherent to all human societies, and the capacity for these laws not be applied in specific cases is intrinsic to their nature as legal precepts. This perspective on equity articulated by Thomas finds resonance among a significant number of Christian and Jewish scholars. The question of equity and the potential influence of Maimonides, as explored in the *Guide for the Perplexed*, III.34, on Thomas's views in this context, will be subject to further investigation in future research endeavors.

adverse circumstances). Geraldus's stance assumes a more ambiguous character than that of the Doctor Angelicus, aligning him more closely with the original Aristotelian text.

In contrast, Rabbi Baruch emerges as an even more staunch proponent of a universal conception of natural law than the Latin commentators. He interprets Thomas's position as positing the existence of inherent distinctions among various conventional laws. This interpretation of Thomas suggests that even within the domain of specific (conventional) laws, certain natural differences exist that render one specific law superior to another, in accordance with the natural objectives of human existence.

Conclusion

In summary, it becomes evident that the historical influence of specific philosophical traditions play a significant role in shaping interpretations of Aristotle's work. Certain developments, such as the distinctions drawn between various categories of natural and conventional laws within the Latin tradition, or the assertion that specific populations may be incapable of adhering to certain aspects of natural law within the Byzantine tradition, are demonstrably influenced by the distinct trajectories of each respective tradition.

Nevertheless, it is noteworthy that within each tradition, philosophers find ample room for the development and articulation of their unique philosophical ideas, while simultaneously grounding them in the text of Aristotle. Notably, the Hebrew, Arabic, and Byzantine traditions have cultivated markedly distinct interpretations of Aristotle's work, building on the tension between relativism and objective natural law. In contrast, within the Latin tradition, the influence of thinkers such as Albertus Magnus and Thomas Aquinas looms more prominently over subsequent generations of scholars. This may be attributed, in part, to the advanced state of development in the discourse on natural law during the Roman period and within canon law.

SECTION THREE

CHAPTER TEN:
NATURAL LAW IN MEDIEVAL JEWISH PHILOSOPHY – A SUMMARY

In this appendix, I aim to provide a concise overview of the discourse on the concept of natural law in medieval Jewish philosophy. As I mentioned in the introductory section of this book, the existing scholarly discussions regarding the relationship between Judaism and the notion of natural law have a tendency to narrow their focus on a limited number of thinkers. Consequently, they tend to present a somewhat homogeneous portrayal of the diverse range of perspectives held by various Jewish philosophers and thinkers on the topic of natural law.

From my vantage point, it is crucial to acknowledge that there exists no singular "Jewish opinion" concerning any specific philosophical matter. Judaism, as a sociological categorization, lacks a distinct philosophical or theological standpoint.[1] Rather, we observe that certain

---

[1] For further exploration of this subject, I recommend the introduction of Sadik 2023. The intricate issue concerning the interplay between Jewish identity and religious identity is multifaceted and evidently exceeds the scope of this discussion. From a personal perspective, Jewish religion primarily relies on practical aspects, and even within the religious and rabbinic trends within Judaism, a consensus on philosophical matters is hard to come by. However, there are certain sacred concepts, such as the unity of God, which although universally accepted, are subject to varying interpretations by different thinkers. These interpretations

philosophical trends gain popularity among specific thinkers such as philosophers, kabbalists, traditionalists, and so on, during specific periods of time. However, it is crucial to note that these trends are historical descriptions rather than essential distinctions, as they are subject to change over time.[2] This observation holds true for the discourse on natural law as well.

In this synopsis, we shall explore the diverse perspectives found in medieval Jewish philosophy concerning the interplay between divine commandments and natural law. Our aim is to present these positions without claiming that they are representive of the predominant trend beyond the medieval era or reflect the thought of all Jewish thinkers, non-philosophers included. We shall observe that medieval Jewish philosophers establish a certain connection between morality and the duty to observe the commandments.[3] This inclination is understandable

---

transcend any prescribed boundaries, rendering these sacred expressions devoid of any philosophical connotations.

[2] I elaborate on this viewpoint in Sadik 2017, which delves into the subject of choice and freedom.

[3] The diverse opinions presented in this summary are grounded in Sadik forthcoming. It is important to note that the scope of this summary does not encompass providing specific texts or engaging in scholarly debates on the opinions of these thinkers. For a more comprehensive exploration of Maimonides' viewpoint, one may also refer to the chapter on natural law Sadik 2023a. This summary predominantly focuses on a specific trend of thinkers from the medieval period, thereby examining a larger number of philosophers than the majority of the book, which aims to elucidate the broader subject of the relationship between Judaism and morality in general.

among religious philosophers who perceive a religious necessity for embracing philosophy and seeking a philosophical basis for religious practice. A significant segment of Jewish philosophers maintains that moral reasoning constitutes an integral component of the primary motivation behind practicing Jewish commandments.

However, in other streams of medieval or modern Jewish thought, including those of non-philosophers, alternative perspectives exist concerning the relationship between morality and the obligation to observe the commandments.

In this concise chapter, we will offer a brief historical introduction followed by an exploration of the various opinions categorized according to philosophical trends rather than a chronological sequence.

First and foremost, it is important to acknowledge that the term "natural law" did not exist in medieval Jewish philosophy prior to the early fifteenth century. This observation holds true for medieval Muslim philosophy as well. As stated in the introduction, the development of the concept of natural law within and Catholic culture was significantly influenced by classical thinkers. Figures such as Cicero and the Roman stoics had a profound impact on early Church Fathers, particularly Augustine, who considered the relationship between natural law, divine law, and revelation as a central philosophical inquiry. These Latin thinkers, however, were not known or studied among Jewish philosophers and intellectuals which explains the delayed engagement with the question of natural law in Jewish philosophy, beginning around the fifteenth century, under the discernible influence of Latin scholasticism. A portion of this influence can be observed in the chapter discussing the Hebrew commentary and translation of the *Nicomachean Ethics*.

Nonetheless, as Burns argues in the case of Aristotle,[4] thinkers can contemplate, write about, and discuss a subject without employing its specific terminology or description. Jewish philosophers and thinkers have extensively addressed topics that are relevant to the question of natural law. For instance, the elucidation of the divine commandments (טעמי המצוות) is directly connected to the question of natural law, and by examining their explanations of the commandments, we can glean insights into these thinkers' perspectives on natural law.

In the period preceding Maimonides,[5] most Jewish thinkers espoused the notion that the commandments could be divided into two categories: those with reasons accessible to rational reflection, and those whose reasons are incomprehensible. This type of distinction existed, albeit with significant variations, in the views of Rabbi Saadia Gaon[6] and Rabbi Yehuda Halevi,[7] Maimonides had a profound impact on later Jewish philosophy, particularly through his proposition that human intellect can discern the reasoning behind all the commandments. In this summary we briefly mentioned how Maimonides' specific stance on natural law is interconnected with his perspective on the rationale behind the commandments.

---

[4] Burns 2011.

[5] Spain, Marroco, Israel and Egypt, 1138-1204.

[6] Egypt, Israel and Babylon, 882-942.

[7] Spain, Egypt and perhaps Israel, 1075-1141.

In the wake of Maimonides, many subsequent thinkers, even those with more conservative views, adopted the belief that every commandment possesses some form of rational explanation. They contended that through rational inquiry, one could discover the underlying rationale behind each commandment.[8]

I will categorize medieval Jewish philosophers based on their opinions rather than following a strict chronological order. These philosophers can be divided into six distinct groups, each presenting a different view on the question of natural law and the Jewish commandments:

1. Philosophers who perceive a complete harmony between natural law and Jewish commandments. According to these thinkers, there exists a clearly discernible natural law that can be comprehended by human intellect. They argue that this universal natural law is entirely synonymous with the commandments as practiced in rabbinical Jewish religion.

2. Philosophers who contend that certain commandments possess explicit rational justifications, while others have reasons that are initially incomprehensible but can be understood after they are given by God or His prophets.

---

[8] There are exceptions as some pre-Maimonidean thinkers do not explicitly mention a division between rational and non-rational commandments. Notably, the Yemenite Jewish philosopher Rabbi Natanel al-Fayyumi (c. 1090-1165) is a significant example. Upon examination, it becomes apparent that he likely held a relativist viewpoint regarding the question of natural law. Additionally, certain post-Maimonidean thinkers, such as Gersonides (1288-1344), also acknowledge this division between commandments based on reason and those that lack rational explanation.

3. Philosophers who maintain that these commandments are akin to natural law. However, they posit that the moral imperative to observe all the commandments is of lesser importance, with the primary impetus lying in the human need to worship God.

4. Rabbi Judah Halevi posits that certain commandments in Jewish law are in alignment with natural morality. These commandments can be comprehended through human intellect and are grounded in rational reasoning. However, there are other commandments that transcend the natural realm and possess supernatural and super-rational justifications. These commandments go beyond the scope of human understanding and cannot be grasped by human intellect alone.

5. Jewish philosophers who adopt a relativist philosophical stance but believe that the Jewish rabbinic commandments possess historical advantages rather than being based on natural law.

6. Philosophers who argue for philosophical equality among different types of law and religions. Even within these two categories, there are limits to the relativist perspective, as not all laws and societies conform entirely to the natural needs of human beings.

In this summary, I will provide the names of the prominent philosophers within each group and highlight some of the key philosophical divergences among them. The primary focus of this summary will be on their philosophical opinions and their relevance to the question of natural law. Given the limitations of a concise appendix in this monograph, I will not be able to provide extensive textual evidence or engage in the scholarly debates surrounding the opinions of these philosophers. Nonetheless, it is my hope that this summary will prove valuable in acquainting English readers with the diverse range of opinions about natural law within medieval Jewish philosophy.

1. Natural law as identical to the divine commandment

A notable group of Jewish philosophers who emerged after Maimonides, including Rabbi Samuel Ibn Tibbon (Provence, 1150-1230), Rabbi Moses Ibn Tibbon (Provence, d. 1283), Rabbi Isaac Pulgar (north Castile, first half of the fourteenth century), Rabbi Levi Ben Avraham (Provence, 1245-1315), Rabbi Moses of Narbonne (Provence and Spain, 1300-1362), Rabbi Joseph Ibn Kaspi (Provence and Spain, 1280-1345), and Rabbi Hoter Ben Shlomo (Yemen, 1400-1480), held the view that Jewish law is entirely synonymous with natural law. Accordingly, natural law encompasses even specific commandments, such as the precise rabbinical laws pertaining to observing Shabbat or adhering to certain dress codes. Apart from Rabbi Hoter Ben Shlomo, most of these philosophers adopt a naturalistic stance and do not believe that prophecy can reveal truths that surpass human intellect or rational capabilities. Consequently, they assert that Moses was the greatest philosopher and that the law he bestowed upon the Jewish people represents the best possible framework for human beings.

Based on their philosophical convictions, these thinkers argue that there exists a type of law that is most suitable for human nature and society. While some among them downplay the significance of historical or cultural distinctions, such as Rabbi Isaac Pulgar, others contend that the Jewish people possess superior natural capacities and a unique historical trajectory, which qualifies them as the sole bearers of the best natural law, as exemplified by Rabbi Levi ben Avraham's viewpoint. What remains consistent among these philosophers is the notion that any deviation from Jewish commandments, such as their modification, constitutes the differentiating factor between other legal systems and natural law.[9] They perceive themselves as carrying on the legacy of Maimonides and do not interpret his position as relativism.

2. Natural law with a distinction between rationally understandable and non-understandable commandments

Three notable Jewish philosophers who espouse this view are Rabbi Saadia Gaon, Rabbi Abraham ben David (Al-Andalus – Muslim Spain, 1110-1180), and Gersonides (Provence, 1288-1344). They argue for a clear differentiation between commandments that are readily comprehensible to regular (non-prophetic) human intellect and those that are not. According to these philosophers, in the realm of clear intellectual understanding, there exists a strong connexion between Jewish commandments and natural law. On the other hand, the remaining commandments are considered conventional and lacking in rationality.[10] This distinction applies not only to specific commandments but also to

---

[9] This opinion derives from Plato's *Republic*, V.449a: Ἀγαθὴν μὲν τοίνυν τὴν τοιαύτην πόλιν τε καὶ πολιτείαν καὶ ὀρθὴν καλῶ, καὶ ἄνδρα τὸν τοιοῦτον· κακὰς δὲ τὰς ἄλλας καὶ ἡμαρτημένας, εἴπερ αὕτη ὀρθή, περί τε πόλεων διοικήσεις καὶ περὶ ἰδιωτῶν ψυχῆς τρόπου κατασκευήν.

[10] The demarcation between the two types of commandments varies among different philosophers.

entire categories, particularly in the opinion of Rabbi Saadia. Nevertheless, even these more specific commandments possess some natural reasoning that renders them superior to others.[11] These nuances are not readily apparent and can only be discerned after the giving of the commandments by Moses. R. Saadia and R. Abraham underscore the religious obligation to observe these commandments, even in the absence of intellectual comprehension of their underlying rationales.

3. Natural law as a minor reason to practice the commandments.

Rabbi Hasdai Crescas (Aragon, 1340-1412), and his student Rabbi Joseph Albo (Aragon and Castile, 1380-1444), offer an alternative explanation regarding the commandments. While they both maintain that Jewish law is synonymous with natural law, their approach builds upon the views of Maimonides (without embracing his notion of relative morality). Rabbi Crescas constructs his rationale for the commandments based on Maimonides' view, emphasizing the demonstration of human love for God through their observance. According to Rabbi Crescas, the practice of the commandments serves to attain perfection and afterlife, displaying human love to God. These commandments, bestowed upon humanity by God, also align with human nature and are beneficial for individuals. Nonetheless, this aspect is considered a secondary reason for fulfilling the

---

[11] According to the perspective of Rabbi Saadia, the specific details of the commandments that are comprehensible fall within the same category. Their rationality becomes clear to us only after we acquire knowledge of them.

commandments. Rabbi Crescas argues that a person facing challenging circumstances, such as Jews forcibly converted to Christianity, may observe fewer commandments but display a deeper love for God compared to a co-religionist in a more favourable situation who practices more commandments but does not have the same level of love for God. In this scenario, the convert is deemed closer to God in both the present world and the afterlife.

Rabbi Albo combines Maimonides' viewpoint with Thomas Aquinas's conception of natural law. The principal distinction between Rabbi Albo and Thomas Aquinas lies in their respective explanations: Rabbi Albo, being a Jewish philosopher, elucidates the reasons behind the superiority of the laws of Moses, while Christian scholastic thinkers, such as Thomas Aquinas, focus on the non-identification of the ceremonial commandments of the Mosaic law with natural law. Similarly, Rabbi Albo posits that the moral and political reasons for observing the commandments represent only a less significant factor in the obligation to follow them. The primary imperative to adhere to the commandment arises from the obligation to fulfill the divine will.

4. Natural law as a reason to practice only some of the commandments.

According to Rabbi Judah Halevi, there is a division, more pronounced than in the thinkers of the second group, between political commandments applicable to all people and nations and ceremonial commandments. The rational capacity of human intellect is insufficient to comprehend the reasons underlying the ceremonial commandments, as their purpose is to cultivate the relationship between humans and the divine, which transcends natural understanding. Any attempt to grasp the workings of the divine in these matters is prone to the development of erroneous theories, which can lead to heresy (as exemplified by the Kabbalists in the two generations following Rabbi Halevi's demise). Even non-Jewish individuals, such as the king of the Khazars described in Rabbi Halevi's book, can recognize the divine providence manifested in the Jewish people and understand that this providence stems from the observance of true supernatural commandments. They can perceive the impact of the ceremonial commandments without comprehending their modus operandi. The Jewish political commandments are congruent with natural law, while the ceremonial commandments constitute a part of nature that is inexplicable. Humans can only apprehend the sacred influence of these commandments without fully grasping their functioning. Thus, these commandments are indeed part of natural law, albeit not in the conventional sense as commonly defined by most individuals.

5. Relativist moral opinion with an historical advantage to the Jewish commandments

Maimonides embraced a moral relativist stance with a historical advantage attributed to Jewish commandments. He made a clear distinction between truth and goodness, asserting that truth pertains to objective physical laws (such as the Earth being round), while goodness is linked to moral norms and habits that vary across societies (e.g., differing definitions of modesty). Within the realm of goodness, multiple and equal laws can exist. In his interpretation of the rationale behind commandments,

Maimonides provided sociological and historical explanations for ceremonial commandments. For instance, the objective of sacrificial rituals is to redirect the customary mode of worship practiced by peoples towards the true God, as expounded in the *Guide for the Perplexed* III.32. These interpretations rendered these laws particularly relevant to the specific historical context of Judaism, distinguishing them from other historical contexts. Due to his relativist moral stance, Maimonides was able to explain commandments that earlier Jewish philosophers (such as Rabbis Saadia and Halevi) viewed as originating from divine, super-natural providence. However, Maimonides envisaged some boundaries to this relativist perspective, claiming that social norms should guide individuals to prioritize their intellect over bodily temptations. Societies that prioritize freedom of bodily pleasure as a major objective would fall outside the legitimate norms of morality, according to Maimonides, who considered drunkenness as contrary to truth, rather than goodness. Maimonides' relativist perspective likely stemmed, in part, from his study of our chapter in the Arabic translation of Aristotle's *Nicomachean Ethics*, which presented Aristotle as more relativist than in the original Greek text.

Nevertheless, Maimonides also maintained that all of humanity shares a common historical background. He further argued that Jewish law is best equipped to address the prevalent historical backdrop of idolatry among all humans. Consequently, the superiority of Jewish law is not directly rooted in natural law and morality, but rather in historical considerations. Rabbi Jacob Anatoli (Provence and Italy, 1194-1256) followed in the footsteps of Maimonides by emphasizing the superiority of Jewish law in relation to history rather than directly pertaining to natural law.

6. Relativist opinion

Two medieval Jewish philosophers, Rabbi Netanel al Fayyumi (Yemen, fl. twelfth century) and Rabbi Isaac Albalag (Provence, end of the thirteenth – beginning of the fourteenth), held a comprehensive relativist and pluralist perspective on morality. These philosophers embraced a relativistic understanding of moral values, asserting that each society and culture requires distinct laws that correspond to its specific historical context. This viewpoint finds its roots in the writings of the Muslim philosopher Abu Nasr al-Farabi (870-950). According to this stance, various religious founders are philosophers who uncover the same philosophical truths and construct laws that align with the history and culture of their respective societies. Notably, these philosophers, particularly Rabbi Albalag, maintain that different religions can be both equal and yet distinct. Nevertheless, he argues that the need for religion is universal across all human societies, as it provides a means to uphold moral norms that are essential for societal well-being.

Conclusion

In this synthesis, we observe that various Jewish medieval philosophers hold distinct perspectives regarding natural law. While they unanimously agree on the obligatory nature of Jewish rabbinic commandments (except for the sixth group of philosophers who limit this obligation to Jews), they are all influenced by the *Nicomachean Ethics*, albeit in different translations. Notably, the relativist inclination is primarily evident among Jewish philosophers with knowledge of the Arabic translation of the *Nicomachean Ethics*, such as Maimonides, and Rabbis Anatoli, Netanel, and Albalag. This suggests a potential impact of this translation on Jewish philosophy. However, certain thinkers who are proficient in Arabic and harbour a more critical stance towards Aristotle in general, such as Rabbi Saadia and Rabbi Halevi, do not adopt a relativist standpoint.[12] The influence of philosophical translations holds significant weight and contributes to the intellectual development of these philosophers. Nevertheless, it represents merely one facet of their development, as they are also influenced by other readings and, most notably, by their own philosophical inquiries, which lead them in entirely divergent directions.

---

[12] It is worth noting that in the philosophical dialogue of Rabbi Halevi, the philosopher expresses a relativist stance. This portrayal is perhaps meant to reflect Aristotle's position as interpreted by Rabbi Halevi.

BIBLIOGRAPHY

Primary sources

Commentary or translation of the Nicomachean Ethics.

Original:

Aristotle's Ethica Nicomachea, J. Bywater (ed.). Oxford 1894.

Arabic:

The Arabic Version of the Nicomachean Ethics, A. Akasoy and A. Fidora (eds.), based on the work of M. Dunlop, Leiden 2005.

English:

Nicomachean Ethics, F. H. Peters (trans.) . London 1906.

Nicomachean Ethics, H. Rackham (trans.), London 1934.

Nicomachean Ethics, W. D. Ross (trans.), London 1925.

French:

Ethique à Nicomaque, J. B. Saint-Hilaire and A. Gomez-Muller (trans.), Paris 1992.

La moral, M. Thurot (trans.), Paris 1824.

Greek:

Eustratii et Michaelis et anonyma In Ethica Nicomachea commentaria, Gustav Heylbut (ed.), Berlin 1892.

Georgios Pachymeres, *Commentary on Aristotle's Nicomachean Ethics*, S. Xenophontos (ed.), Berlin 2022.

Michaelis Ephesii in librum quintum Ethicorum Nicomacheorum commentarium, Berlin 1901.

Hebrew:

Rabbi Baruch ben Yaish's translation: Hamburg, Staats- und Universitatsbibliothek, ms. Levy 114.

R. Meir Alguadez' translation in: C. Neria, *"It Cannot Be Valued with the Gold of Ophir" (Job 28:16): Rabbi Joseph b. Shem-Ṭob's Commetarry on Aristotle's Nicomachean Ethics. Sources and Analysis,* PhD Thesis, University of Chicago, Chicago 2015, pp. 411-566.

Averroes' Middle Commentary on Aristotle's Nicomachean Ethics in the Hebrew Version of Samuel Ben Judah, L. W. Berman (ed.), Jerusalem 1999.

Rabbi Baruch Ibn Ya'ish's Commentary: Paris, Bibliothèque nationale de France, ms. Hebrew 1001, 1002 and 1003.

Rabbi Joseph ibn Kaspi, *Trumat Ha Kessef (The Donation of Silver)*: Wien, Österreichische Nationalbibliothek, cod. Hebr. 27.

The Commentary of Joseph ibn Shem-Tov: 1. Paris, Bibliothèque nationale de France, ms. Hébreu 996 (from Kaufmann 14681); 2. Moscow, Russian State Library, ms. Günzburg 542 (from Kaufmann 17381); 3. Paris, Bibliothèque nationale de France, ms. Hébreu 997 (from Kaufmann 14682).

Latin:

Thomas Aquinas, *In decem Libros ethicorum Aristotelis ad Nicomachum expositio*, R. M. Spiazzi (ed.), Rome 1949. (The volume also contains the translation by Grosseteste and William of Moerbeke translation).

Aristotelis Stagyritae Ethicorum lib. X, Leonardo Bruni (trans.), Venice 1542.

Albertus Magnus, *Opera Omnia*, A. Borgnet (ed.), Paris 1890–1899, vol. VII (1891).

Jean Buridan, *Quaestiones super decem libros Ethicorum Aristotelis*, Paris 1513, transcribed by F. Pironet, *Questions sur l'Ethique à Nicomaque*.

Geraldus Odonis, *Commentarius in Aristotelis Ethicam*, Venice 1500.

Radulphus Brito, *Quaestiones in Aristotelis libros Ethicorum*, Iacopo Costa (ed.), Leiden 2008.

Other sources

Albertus Magnus, *De bono*, in *Opera Omnia*, A. Borgnet (ed.), Paris 1890–1899.

Al-Farabi, *Abū Nasr al-Fārābīs: Mabādī ārā' ahl al-madīna al-fāḍila. A Revised Text with Introduction, Translation, and Commentary*, Richard Walzer (ed.), Oxford 1985.

Al-Farabi, *Kitab as-Siysah al-Madinyah*, Beyrout 2012.

Cicero, *De legibus*, https://www.thelatinlibrary.com/cicero/leg.

Cicero, *De republica*, https://www.thelatinlibrary.com/cicero/repub.

Josef Albo, *Sefer ha-'Ikkarim* [Book of Principles], I. Husik (trans. and ed.), Philadelphia, 1929.

Maimonides, *Guide for the Perplexed*, S. Pines (trans.), Chicago 1963.

Plato, *Respublica*, in *Platonis Opera*, J. Burnet (ed.), vol. IV: *Tetralogia VIII*, Oxford 1903, pp. 327-621.

Plato, *The Republic,* in *Plato in Twelve Volumes,* voll. V & VI, Paul Shorey (trans.), London, 1969.

Thomas Aquinas, *Summa Theologiae*, https://www.corpusthomisticum.org/

Secondary sources

Aouad and Woerther 2009 = M. Aouad and F. Woerther, "Le commentaire par Averroès du chapitre 9 du livre X de l'Éthique à Nicomaque: pédagogie de la contrainte, habitudes et lois", *Mélanges de l'Université Saint-Joseph* 62 (2009), pp. 353-380.

Arabic Version = *The Arabic Version of the Nicomachean Ethics*, Anna A. Akasoy, Alexander Fidora, and Douglas M. Dunlop (eds.), Leiden 2005.

Aslanov 2002 = C. Aslanov, "L'aristotélisme médiéval au service du commentaire littéral: Le cas de Joseph Caspi", *Revue des Etudes Juives* 161 (2002), pp. 123-137.

Asmis 2008 = E. Asmis, "Cicero on Natural Law and the Laws of the State", *Classical Antiquity* 27 (2008), pp. 1-33.

Barber and Jenkins 2009 = C. Barber and D. Jenkins (eds), *Medieval Greek Commentaries on the Nicomachean Ethics*. Leiden, 2009.

Ben-Shalom 2010 = R. Ben-Shalom, "The Diary of the Journey to the East of Josef Ibn Kaspi (Unwritten)", *Pa'amim* 124 (2010), pp. 51-57.

Berman 1967 = L. Berman, "Excerpts from the Lost Arabic Original of Ibn Rushd's *Middle Commentary* on the *Nicomachean Ethics*", *Oriens* XX (1967), pp. 31-59.

Berman 1988 = L. Berman, "The Latin-to-Hebrew Translation of the *Nicomachean Ethics*", *Meḥḳere Yerushalayim be-maḥashevet Yiśra'el* 7 (1988), pp. 147-168.

Berman 1999 = *Averroes' Middle Commentary on Aristotle's Nicomachean Ethics in the Hebrew Version of Samuel Ben Judah*, L. W. Berman (ed.), Jerusalem 1999.

Botley 2004 = P. Botley, *Latin Translation of the Renaissance: The Theory and Practice of Leonardo Bruni, Ginnozzo Manetti, and Desiderius Erasmus*. Cambridge 2004.

Brown 1977 = L. Brown, "What is the 'mean relative to us' in Aristotle's Ethics?", *Phronesis* 42 (1997), pp. 77-93.

Burns 2011 = T. Burns, *Aristotle and Natural Law*, New York 2011.

Callus 1947 = D. Callus, "The Date of Grosseteste's Translations and Commentaries on Pseudo-Dionysius and the Nicomachean Ethics", *Recherches de Théologie Ancienne et Médiévale* 14 (1947), pp. 186–209.

Cohen 2015 = M. Cohen, "Josef Ibn Kaspi: New Biographical Data," *Pa'amim* 145 (2015), pp. 143-166 (in Hebrew).

Corbett 2009 = R. J. Corbett, "The Question of Natural Law in Aristotle", *History of Political Thought* 30 (2009), pp. 229-250.

Costa 2012 = I. Costa, 'L'"Éthique à Nicomaque" à la faculté des arts de Paris avant et après 1277', *Archives d'histoire doctrinale et littéraire du Moyen Age* 79 (2012), pp. 71-114.

Cunningham 1967 = S. B. Cunningham, "Albertus Magnus on Natural Law," *The Journal of the History of Ideas* 28 (1967), pp. 479-502.

Curzer 1996 = H. Curzer, "A Defense of Aristotle's Doctrine of the Mean", *Ancient Philosophy* 16 (1996), pp. 129-138.

David 2010 = J. E. David, "Maimonides: Nature and Natural Law", *Journal of Law, Philosophy and Culture* V (2010), pp. 67-82.

Destree 2000 = P. Destree, "Aristote et la Question du droit naturel", *Phronesis* 45 (2000), pp. 220-238.

Deuffic 2002 = J.-L. Deuffic, "Un logicien renommé, proviseur de Sorbonne au XIVe siècle: Raoul le Breton de Ploudiry. Notes bio-bibliographiques," *Pecia. Ressources en médiévistique* 1 (2002), pp. 145–154.

Ducke 2020 = G. Ducke, "Aristotle and Natual Law", *The Review of Politics* 82 (2020), pp. 1-23.

Dunbadin 1972 = L. Dunbadin, "Robert Grosseteste as Translator, Transmitter, and Commentator: The "Nicomachean Ethics"', *Traditio* 28 (1972), pp. 460-472.

Emon, Levering and Novak 2014 = A. Emon, M. Levering, and D. Novak, *Natural Law: A Jewish, Christian, and Islamic Trialogue,* New York 2014.

Ehrlich 2006 = D. Ehrlich. "A Reassessment of Natural Law in Rabbi Joseph Albo's 'Book of Principles'", *Hebraic Political Studies* 1 (2006), pp. 413-439

Fox 1972 = M. Fox. "Maimonides and Aquinas on Natural Law", *Dine Israel* 3 (1972), pp. v-xxxvi.

Fuchs 2017 = M. J. Fuchs, *Gerechtigkeit als allgemeine Tugend: Die Rezeption der aristotelischen Gerechtigkeitstheorie im Mittelalter und das Problem des ethischen Universalismus,* Berlin 2017.

García-Huidobro 2015 = J. García-Huidobro, "La recepción de la doctrina aristotélica de la justicia natural por Buridan", *Revista de estudios histórico-jurídicos* 37 (2015), pp. 429-452.

Gauthier 1948 = R. A. Gauthier, "Trois Commentaires 'Averroïstes' sur l'Ethique à Nicomaque", *Archives d'Histoire Doctrinale Et Littéraire du Moyen Âge* 16 (1947-1948), pp. 187-336

J. Guttman 1913 = J. Guttman, "Die Familie Schemtob in ihren Beziehungen zur Philosophie", *Monatsschrift für Geschichte und Wissenschaft des Judentums* 57(1913), pp. 447-451.

Guttman 1955 = J. Guttmann, "An Inquiry Concerning the Sources of the *Sefer ha-Ikkarim*", In: *On Repentance and Redemption: Presented to Binyamin Gross,* D. Schwartz and A. Gross (eds), Jerusalem 1955, pp. 169–191 (in Hebrew).

Halper 2010 = Y. Halper, *Averroes on Metaphysical Terminology: An Analysis and Critical Edition of the Long Commentary on Aristotle's Metaphysics Δ*, PhD thesis, Bar Ilan 2010.

Hardie 1987 = W. F. R. Hardie, "Aristotle's Doctrine that Virtue is a 'Mean'", *Meeting of the Aristotelian Society* (1965), pp. 183-204.

Hayoun 1991 = M. Hayoun and A. De Libera, *Averroès et l'averroïsme*, Paris 1991.

Herring 1982 = B. Herring, *Joseph Ibn Kaspi's Geviea Kesef, A Study in Medieval Jewish Philosophic Bible Commentary*, New York 1982, pp. 3-32.

Hursthouse 1980-1981 = R. Hursthouse, "A False Doctrine of the Mean", *Proceeding of the Aristotelian Society* 81 (1980-1981), pp. 57-72.

Jacobs 2010 = J. Jacobs, *Law, Reason, and Morality in Medieval Jewish Philosophy*, Oxford 2010.

Kasher 1982 = H. Kasher, *Josef Ibn Kaspi as an Exegete-Philosopher*, Ph.D. dissertation, Bar Ilan University, Ramat Gan 1982 (in Hebrew).

Kasher 2006 = H Kasher, *Introduction to Shulchan Kessef (Silver Table),* Jerusalem 2006.

Koehn 2012 = G. Koehn, "The Archer and Aristotle's Doctrine of the Mean", *Peitho – Examina Antiqua* 3 (2012), pp. 155-167.

Le Blanc 2008 = L. Bruni, *De interpretatione recta. De la traduction parfaite*, trans. C. Le Blanc, Ottawa 2008.

Lerner 1964 = R. Lerner, "Natural Law in Albo's *Book of Roots*", in *Ancients and Moderns: Essays on the Tradition of Political Philosophy in Honor of Leo Strauss*, J. Cropsey (ed.), New York 1964, pp. 132–147.

Loberbaum 2002 = M. Loberbaum, *Politics and the Limits of Law: Secularizing the Political in Medieval Jewish Thought*, Stanford 2002.

Losin 1987 = P. Losin, "Aristotle's Doctrine of the Mean", *History of Philosophy Quarterly* 4 (1987), pp. 329-341.

Lisska 1997 = A. Lisska, *Aquinas's Theory of Natural Law: An Analytic Reconstruction*, Oxford 1997.

Luscombe 1982 = D. E. Luscombe, "Natural Morality and Natural Law," in *The Cambridge History of Later Medieval Philosophy*, N. Kretzmann, A. Kenny, and J. Pinborg (eds.), Cambridge 1982, pp. 705-720

MacIntyre 1981 = Alasdair MacIntyre, *After Virtue: A Study in Moral Theology*, Notre Dame 1981.

Melamed 1986 = A. Melamed, "Natural Law in Medieval and Renaissance Jewish Political Thought" (Hebrew), *Daat* 17 (1986), pp. 49-66.

Mesch 1975 = B. Mesch, *Studies in Josef Ibn Kaspi, Fourteenth-Century Philosopher and Exegete*, Leiden 1975, pp. 43-59.

Neria 2015 = C. Neria , *It Cannot Be Valued With The Gold Of Ophir" (Job 28:16): Rabbi Joseph B. Shem-Ṭob's Commetarry on Aristotle's Nicomachean Ethics — Sources and Analysis*, PhD Thesis, University of Chicago, Chicago 2015.

Novak 1998 = D. Novak, *Natural Law in Judaism*, Cambridge 1998.

Oates 1936 = W. J. Oates, "The Doctrine of the Mean", *The Philosophical Review* 45 (1936), pp. 382-398.

Olfert 2014 = C. M. M. Olfert, "Aristotle's Conception of Practical Truth", *Journal of the History of Philosophy* 52 (2014), pp. 205-231.

Poblete 2018 = J. Poblete, "Translation or Alteration? Grosseteste's Latin Version of Aristotle's Account of

Natural Justice", *Journal of the History of Philosophy* 54 (2018), pp. 601-628.

Poblete 2020 = J. Poblete, "The Medieval Reception of Aristotle's Passage on Natural Justice the Role of Grosseteste's Latin Translation of Ethica Nicomachea", *American Catholic Philosophical Quarterly* 94 (2020), pp. 211-238.

Porti 2017 = D. Porti, *Shem Tov ben Joseph Ibn Shem Tov and his Commentary on the Guide for the Perplexed by Maimonides,* PhD Thesis, Ben-Gurion University of the Negev, Beersheba 2017.

Ragev 1993 = S. Ragev, *Theology and Rationalist Mysticism in the Writings of Rabbi Joseph Ibn Shem Tov,* PhD Thesis, Hebrew University, Jerusalem 1993.

Rak 2007 = I. Rak, *The Biblical Interpretation of Rabbi Josef Ibn Kaspi: Methods of Interpretation and an Elaborated Scientific Edition of Mezaref LeKessef (Inclusive to Genesis),* Ph.D. dissertation, Bar-Ilan University, Ramat Gan 2007.

Renan 1925 = E. Renan, *Averroès et l'averroïsme: essai historique,* Paris 1925.

Rothschild 2011 = Jean-Pierre Rothschild, "La contestation des fins de la politique selon Aristote chez quelques auteurs juifs du moyen âge tardif en Espagne", in: *Well Begun is Only Half Done: Tracing Aristotle's Political Ideas in Medieval Arabic, Syriac, Byzantine, and Jewish Sources,* V. Syros (ed.), Tempe, 2011, pp. 187-221.

Rothschild 2016 = J. P. Rothschild, "L'appropriation de *l'Éthique à Nicomaque* par le judaïsme espagnol: le travail des préfaces (Me'ir Alguadez, Joseph ben Shem Tob Ibn Shem Tob)", *Ibéria Judaica* 8 (2016), pp. 61-122.

Rudavsky 2012 = T. Rudavsky, "Natural Law in Judaism a Reconsideration", in *Reason, Religion and Natural Law*, J. A. Jacobs (ed.), Oxford 2012, pp. 83-105.

Saccenti 2001 = R. Saccenti, *Debating Medieval Natural Law – A Survey,* Notre Dame 2016;

Tierney 2001 = B. Tierney, *The Idea of Natural Rights: Studies on Natural Rights, Natural Law, and Church Law, 1150-1625*, Grand Rapids 2001.

Sackson 2016 = A. Sackson, *Josef Ibn Kaspi, Portrait of a Hebrew Philosopher in Medieval Provence*, PhD dissertation, New York 2016.

Sadik 2017 = S. Sadik, "Natural Morality in the Thought of R. Josef Ibn Kaspi", *Daat* 83 (2017), pp. 161-174.

Sadik 2017' = S. Sadik, *The Essence of Choice in Medieval Jewish Philosophy*, Jerusalem 2017.

Sadik 2021 = S. Sadik, "The Meaning of 'מפורסמות' in the Thought of Maimonides and his Philosophical Sources," *JSIJ* 20 (2021), forthcoming.

Sadik 2023 = S. Sadik, "Equity and Law in the Hebrew Commentaries of the Nicomachean Ethics", *Jewish Law Annual* 23 (2024), forthcoming.

Sadik 2023a = S. Sadik, *Maimonides: A Radical Religious Philosopher*, Gorgias Press 2023.

Sadik forthcoming = S. Sadik, *Reason of the Commandment and Natural Law in Medieval Jewish Philosophy*, forthcoming.

Sagi 1998 = A. Sagi, *Judaism: Between Religion and Morality*, Jerusalem 1998 (in Hebrew).

Sirat 1983 = C. Sirat, *La philosophie juive au Moyen Age, Selon les textes manuscrits et imprimés*, (C.N.R.S.) Paris 1983, Tome II *La philosophie juive médiévale en pays de Chrétienté.*

Strauss 1999 = L. Strauss, *Natural Right and History*, Chicago 1999 (revised edition; first published 1965).

Sweeney 2012 = E. C. Sweeney, "Thomas Aquinas on the Natural Law Written on Our Heart", in *Reason, Religion and Natural Law*, J. A. Jacobs (ed.), Oxford 2012, pp. 133-154.

Taliaferro 2017 = K. Taliaferro, "Ibn Rushd and Natural Law: Mediating Human and Divine Law", *Journal of Islamic Studies* 28 (2017), pp. 1–27.

Tierney 2001 = B. Tierney, *The Idea of Natural Right: Studies on Natural Right, Natural Law, and Church Law 1150-1625*, Grand Rapids 2001.

Tirosh-Samuelson 2003 = H. Tirosh-Samuelson, *Happiness in Premodern Judaism: Virtue, Knowledge and Well-Being*, Cincinnati 2003.

Ullmann 2012 = M. Ullmann *Die Nikomachische Ethik des Aristoteles in arabischer Übersetzung*, Wiessbaden 2012.

Urmson 1973 = J. O. Urmson, "Aristotle's Doctrine of the Mean", *American Philosophical Quarterly* 10 (1973), pp. 223-330.

Urvoy 1988 = D. Urvoy, *Averroès: les ambitions d'un intellectuel musulman*, Mayenne 1998.

von Leyden 1967 = W. von Leyden, "Aristotle and the Concept of Law", *The Journal of the Royal Institute of Philosophy* 62 (1967), pp. 1-19.

Yack 1990 = B. Yack, "Natural Right and Aristotle's Understanding of Justice", *Political Theory* 18 (1990), pp. 216-237.

Wieland 1982 = G. Wieland, "The Reception and Interpretation of Aristotle's Ethics", in *The Cambridge History of Later Medieval Philosophy*, N. Kretzmann, A. Kenny, and J. Pinborg (eds.), Cambridge 1982, pp. 657-672.

Woerther 2019 = F. Woerther, "Les fragments arabes du Commentaire moyen d'Averroès à l'Éthique à Nicomaque'", *Oriens* 47 (2019), pp. 244-312.

Xenophontos 2022 = G.Pachymeres, *Commentary on Aristotle, Nicomachean Ethics*, S. Xenophontos (ed.), Berlin 2022.

Zonta 2006 = M. Zonta, *Hebrew Scholasticism in the Fifteenth Century*, Dordrecht 2006.

www.ingramcontent.com/pod-product-compliance
Lightning Source LLC
Chambersburg PA
CBHW080803300426
44114CB00020B/2807